Selected Poems

DAWSON JACKSON (1910–1994) was educated at Oxford, where he read History. He spent his life writing poetry and working as a translator from Russian and French. His published books include *Against Destruction*, *A Primer of Necessary Belief* and *Abidjan West Africa: a poem*.

NICOLA SIMPSON is Head of English at Abbey College, a sixth-form college in Manchester. She is currently writing her Ph.D. thesis on the concrete poet Dom Sylvester Houdedard at the Manchester Metropolitan University. She has contributed articles and reviews on contemporary poetry to periodicals including *PN Review* and *Stand*.

DAWSON JACKSON

Selected Poems

**edited with an introduction by
Nicola Simpson**

Published by
LILSTOCK PRESS
in association with
CARCANET PRESS

First published in 2002 by

Lilstock Press
in association with
Carcanet Press Limited
4th Floor, Conavon Court
12–16 Blackfriars Street
Manchester M3 5BQ

A CIP catalogue record for this book
is available from the British Library
ISBN trade paperback edition 1 85754 615 6

The publisher acknowledges financial assistance
from the Arts Council of England

Set in Monotype Ehrhardt by XL Publishing Services, Tiverton
Printed and bound in England by SRP Ltd, Exeter

Contents

Introduction

> *a casual, colonial, conversational*
> *look, like Whitman's open shirt and hat.*

Dawson Jackson epitomises his own poetry in these lines from the poem *New York*. They apply to the poet, the undergraduate, controversially traversing the streets of 1920s' Oxford, with long hair, sandals and a buttonless shirt; and to the poems, with their short prosody, in many ways much indebted to Walt Whitman's long lines. The poems *look*, look into the being of things, with words clear, *casual* and insistently *conversational*. Yet the diction on occasions is unconsciously that of the unmistakably English *colonial* voice of one whose childhood was spent in a middle-class family, in the suburbs of Liverpool, at the end of the Victorian age.

Born in Wallasey in 1910, James Dawson Jackson was the second of four children. His family was comfortably off but not rich. In *Tropical Africa* he recalls a grandfather 'in amiable bedroom slippers, white imperial, / Gold pince-nez and a / Skullcap' who perhaps made the small family fortune in the early Victorian advances into colonial Nigeria. However such genealogical details are sparse and as Jackson writes in this poem,

> My family's history
> Is as obscure
> As Africa's.

He was educated at Oundle public school, at the wish of his accountant father, who insisted that a good education was the only inheritance worth having. He then went up to Oxford at the age of 17 to read Modern History at Christ Church. Though a contemporary of W.H. Auden at Oxford, Jackson could not be further away from the Auden Generation in style and manner. He rejected the poetic agenda of his contemporaries, who, writing like 'clerks',

> think that the world is such a disjointed place, even fundamentally, that to be entirely unintelligible and cut off, is quite to be expected. Here I disagree with them; and that is one aspect of why I am not a 'modern poet' [...] each stanza and poem of modern poetry ends with its mouth hanging open[1]

'Unity' was Jackson's answer to this 'disjointed place of Modern Poetry'; a unity which saw no separation between inner and outer worlds, between subjective and objective, between the poetry, the philosophy and the private life of the poet. No aspect of his life was beyond the reach of his poetry, and in particular the women in his life provided a continuous muse that inspired his work.

Spurning the advances of the poet Stephen Spender, a fellow student at Christ Church, Jackson chose to defy convention, on graduating with a first class degree, by living unmarried with the painter and potter Marial Russell. Poems such as 'First Love Making', 'Remembrance of Venus' and 'Reluctant Divinity' recall the eroticism and tenderness of this early relationship.

> She was a sea.
>
> Darkness of that
> Bed: room: cottage:
> Night.   Like the full
> Lingering moon, for
> The first time
> My mouth met
> Lips' rose
> In a kiss.   So
>
> Began
> My freedom:[…][2]

The alliance, however, did not last, and Jackson later married his long-term friend and fellow Oxford graduate, the poet Phoebe Ashburner.

Early married life for the Jacksons was hard. The concept of wealth was anathema to the young poet and a life of severe economy was of paramount importance. In the midst of the 1930s depression Jackson wrote what could be described as libertarian-anarchist apothegms out of the blazing anger that he felt observing the social and economic injustice around him. Proudhon inspired the following:

> Property
> Is a double
> Theft. From
> The thing
> Itself and its full
> Relation to
> Us, and
> From its full
> Relation to
> Others[3]

This anarchist economic view developed over time into a more expansive and complex ecological doctrine, years ahead of the Green movement. In poems such as 'The Blind Suicide', the reader is presented with anti-consumerist argument where humanity is

> [...] helpless to
> Control the
> Tiger of the trivial
> Desires that we are
> Mounted on, which will
> Devour all
> Living things
> Progressively, and
> Us?

After decades of his work being marginalised into counter-culture pamphlets and small magazines, in the 1980s Jackson finally found a wider audience for his progressive economic and ecological message and his treatise *Against Destruction* was well received on its publication in 1984.[4]

Back in the 1930s, however, such progressive thinking was at best eccentric and at worst revolutionary to the neighbours of the newly-weds. In a succession of tiny rented cottages in Somerset, the Jacksons practised a life of self-sufficiency, growing most of their own food and virtually bartering for other provisions they needed. Clothes were low down on the list of necessities, and Jackson's appearance was unconventional for one of his education and background. Sitting on the platform waiting for his train to arrive he would find coins drop into his lap to 'help the refugee'. On other occasions, his long pointed beard, unkempt hair, severe cheekbones and assortment of practical yet eclectic clothing would mean only one thing to the Trotsky-fearing London policemen – that Jackson was a Russian spy.

The birth of the Jacksons' daughter Unity in 1937 led them to look for other work to supplement their income. An opportunity arose for Jackson to translate for his friend Charles Elton, who ran an ecological research bureau in Oxford. This meant learning Russian and, being self-confessedly bad at languages (he nearly failed to get into Oxford on account of his poor Latin and Greek), it posed rather a challenge. Characteristically his single-mindedness won through and within six months he was earning nine pence an hour for his translation work.

Marriage, fatherhood, learning Russian and the paring back of his lifestyle to austere simplicity transformed his poetry from unpublished juvenilia of 'unpresentable' verse to a 'presentable' verse[5] that found its way into periodicals such as the *New Statesman* and *Adelphi*. Despite his own

ix

feelings about the new accessibility of his writing, publishing success remained limited. Max Plowman, editor of *Adelphi*, was a constant source of encouragement and criticism to the young poet. From the outset Plowman was troubled by how 'out of step' with contemporary verse Jackson's style and content were. 'You do not', Plowman wrote, 'find it easy to trust your reader to come and meet you'.[6] Jackson was undeterred by this absence of immediate audience and continued developing a unique philosophical and poetic message that was to find full expression twenty years later in his prose work, *A Primer of Necessary Belief*.[7] To him the message of existence was clear:'It is all souls or none'.[8] One's own existence can not be separated from the existence of all other beings. 'I become what in eternity I am, when I love all of every other thing: and they reply. This makes a single whole, which each – most distinct – is.'[9]

With such philosophical and personal beliefs, it was inevitable that Jackson should be a conscientious objector when war broke out in 1939. His diary of the period recounts the wonderfully comic scene in the courtroom when, trying to ascertain Jackson's occupation, the authorities refused to register the word 'poet'.[10] He could be an artist, a musician, a painter, a potter, a novelist, but not a poet. 'Translator and keeper of six hens' was the National Register's final word on the subject. Looking after hens and cabbages on his smallholding may have been his job to the clerks in the courtroom but, as the same diary asserts, Jackson never lost sight of his true vocation:

> In your spare time from being a poet you can do plenty of jobs as a hobby. But you can't write poetry in your spare time. It has to be your real job, and the best part of your ordinary attention must be left free for it and its demands.[11]

In this 'spare time', after the war, Jackson went on to spend a lifetime working for a variety of acronymic organisations such as the UN, OECD, WHO, FAO, UNESCO, ILO, ITU, translating Russian and French. Never working for more than four or five months of the year on his 'hobby' of translation, he spent the rest of the year immersed in his true task of writing poetry. As a translator he had to travel, and this constantly fed into his poetic work, providing him with many opportunities to continue on the spiritual journey he had so clearly and idealistically outlined at the age of twenty-five:

> I see many horizons, all opening up to me, and I passing over great distances among them. My object and necessity will be to discover, in myself and the outside, the spiritual organisation of the world, in its

breadth (of distance and different kinds of men) and in its depth of poverty, both materially and spiritually.

The poems born of these experiences; *Abidjan, Time Suspended in Tropical Africa, Delhi, New York, Spring Beneath the Alps* and 'L'Aiguille du Midi', are so much more than simply travel poems. They are journeys; spiritual journeys into 'the foreignness and humanity'[12] of each new person and place that he encounters. Years before the hippie trail in the psyche-delic 1960s, Dawson Jackson can be found in India, cycling through the dusty towns, steering around the obstacles of stray cows with his flapping white cotton robes and sage-like beard, journeying into the very heart of the dust and ancient peace of the country. Or in Africa: Abidjan, Kenya, Ghana, Nigeria … journeying into the deepest forest in search of an Africa preserved from the 'civilising' forces of colonialism, an Africa that can re-emerge in the face of independence and flourish and grow once again. Even in *New York*, Jackson journeys along the Hudson,

> To the time when it was
> Comprehensible – by the Indians
> Whose life, and understanding,
> Took form in
> Its mould. The Indians
>
> Have been drowned out
> By our European flood
> From the Atlantic – and in
> Their depth is lost
> The only human key this
> Landscape ever had.

All these journeys are solitary. On each occasion Jackson is alone, unteth-ered from his family and other close personal relationships. After divorcing Phoebe, Jackson married his long-term companion, the radio actress Joan Hart in 1955. Although Joan visited Jackson occasionally abroad, in all the poems there is the sense of the archetypal solitary romantic wanderer. Again the *spiritual journey* that Jackson outlined in his youth provides a template for the experience he strives for in these poems:

For this journey I should have to abandon my personality, and there with all personal feelings, all interest in the universe in its touching of myself, all personal friendships and man-woman love, all home and possession, all thought of the future, all care and concern with myself. Instead I should have to project myself, entirely into the outside world

xi

and people, becoming a pure mirror of the spirit moving within them, so that everything can be a medium to me, I must be only an entity conveying a blessing and message of joy and light and wisdom.

Such journeying continued for over forty years. Throughout his middle and old age his life clearly divided into two halves: the domestic intimacy of the home-life he shared with Joan in St John's Wood, London, until her death in 1984 and the life of global travel that inspired and consolidated his spiritual understanding of the world.

Until his own death in 1994, Dawson Jackson never quit his true occupation. He wrote prolifically for almost seventy years and the body of work he left is vast: over 10,000 pages of verse and volumes of prose. The generosity of spirit, idealism and philosophical determination that he fostered, amongst the home-grown cabbages and six hens, in his early writing career never deserted him. On each page, there is a tangible sense of the struggle to present a 'blessing and message of joy and light and wisdom'.

It is impossible to read the poems and not come to know the man Dawson Jackson. Nowhere are his views mediated through a constructed persona: the autobiographical voice speaks clearly in each poem. In the first section of this book, 'Journeys', the reader follows Jackson around the globe, sharing in his perceptions and spiritual experiences. The second, 'Love', collects some of his most moving and sensual love poems, from the youthful ardour of the clandestine 'marriage' to Marial Russell, through to the tender relationship of his final years. The third section, 'Being', presents the short lyrical poems that best express Jackson's philosophical ideas and moments of insight. The final section draws together those poems that deal with Jackson's recurrent interest and philosophical quest, the truth of 'Death'. In the words of Walt Whitman, 'Who touches this book touches a man.'[13]

Why, in spite of such a prolific and long writing career, did so few of Jackson's works reach an audience? As he writes in the poem 'The Gift',[14] towards the end of his life:

> I wanted to give a
> Present to the world, that thing
> More precious than
> All else I
> Know: pearl
> From the bottom

Of my
Self's
Sea – diamond from this
Dark earth's
Bemusing mine.

Fifty-five years later
Here I am still
Virtually complete – and
Clearly enough, as
From the first I
Knew was
Likely, the world
Does not
Accept it.   I
Got the twentieth
Publisher's refusal
Of my last
Ten years' work today.

The door is shut.

He had small successes with his two early prose titles, *From This Foundation,* and *A Primer of Necessary Belief* and with his later prose work *Against Destruction.* But the audience for his verse remained restricted to the odd poetry magazine and the family and friends who received copies of his self-published collections. What exactly did Max Plowman mean when he commented, early in the poet's career, that Jackson did not readily meet his audience? How had the door shut and had he shut it?

Certainly he did not readily meet his fellow contemporary poets or mix in literary circles. He felt poetically and philosophically removed from the main trends of twentieth-century Modernism. Few contemporary poets interested him. The shaping influences on his early work were Shelley, Blake and Whitman. In self-imposed exile from the poetry scene, Jackson freed himself to develop his own voice in answer to these earlier voices.

Blake and Whitman affected me strongly. From Whitman I took the long line, or Whitman allowed me to take it. Comically enough this later turned, with me, into the very short line.
Blake the vision, Whitman the visualness.[15]

What shut readers out was not the vision, radical though it was, but the visual quality of the poems. Jackson believed his formal experiments would

xiii

lead to the discovery of a verse form that would reflect his vision. 'I need to catch something (a vehicle) to put all this force in.'[16] But the very short line that Jackson developed from Whitman's long line, something to contain the force, the vision, caused a visual impasse for his potential audience. Readers frequently asked Jackson how his poems were meant to *sound*, mistakenly pausing at the end of each line. To do this makes reading any one of his poems a tedious and cumbersome process. Readers familiar with the poetry of William Carlos Williams do not pause at the line break; the lines of Jackson's verse resist such halting enunciation. The end of the line should only be 'a slight trip effect on the eye', a micro-pause more visual than aural. The line breaks function like a typographical punctuation, not too far removed from the visual experiments of American Objectivism.

A helpful analogy for understanding how the lines work is suggested by Michael Schmidt in the Afterword to Jackson's novel-length poem *Abidjan:* 'It's an insistent mode of notation, playing now with and now against the flow of syntax like musical notation, allocating time and value to different phrases and words.'[17] The way this 'musical notation' works can effectively be demonstrated in a passage from the poem *Spring Beneath the Alps.* Here, the structural musicality of the form is fully exploited by the poet to emphasise the music of the nightingale's singing. Of course Jackson was aware of the traditional Romantic metaphor of the Nightingale and his song representing the poet himself and his verse:

> Violins; and
> The full
> Cello: O, O, O.
> And bubblings, bickerings
> Of black
> Notes (this hedge of
> Trees is a long
> Line of music
> Thickly scored), the splashing
> Of bright deep
> Water over stones; and there
> Again the deep
> Pool, the still
> O, O, O, O again
> Repeated, the deep
> Full note.

The verse form is not free but unmetered. Instead of using the beginning of a new line to mark the beginning of a set rhythmic phrase roughly corresponding to syntax and grammar, Jackson uses the lineation to mark *stress* patterns. These stresses play between the beginnings and the end of the line, with the beginnings of lines usually carrying the heaviest stress. So scansion would reveal the following rhythmic pattern:

> /
> Violins; and
>   /
> The full
> / / / /
> Cello: O, O, O.
>   /   / /
> And bubblings, bickerings
> /
> Of black
> /   /
> Notes (this hedge of
> /   /
> Trees is a long
> /   /
> Line of music
> /   /
> Thickly scored), the splashing
> /   /   /
> Of bright deep
> / /
> Water over stones; and there
> /   /
> Again the deep
> / / / / /
> Pool, the still
> / / / / /
> O, O, O, O again
> /   /
> Repeated, the deep
> / /
> Full note.

The stress pattern is not a defined metre but the sounds of the words build up their own internal momentum through a number of repetitious devices. Alliteration, fitting snugly with the stresses, recalls the techniques of Anglo-Saxon and medieval poetry. '*B*ubblings', '*b*ickerings' and '*b*lack' create a rhythmical plosive phrase, which is echoed later in '*b*right' and then varied in the triple repetition of the plosive 'dee*p*'. Similarly, the consonantal music in 'vio*l*ins', 'fu*ll*', 'ce*l*lo' and 'bubb*l*ings', is developed into the full alliterative '*l*ong / *l*ine' before returning to a consonantal patterning in 'sp*l*ashing', 'sti*ll*' and 'fu*ll*'. The starkly alliterative 'O, O, O' is phonologically repeated in 'cell*o*' and 'O,O,O,O' but also visually repeated in the words '*o*f', 'sc*o*red', 'l*o*ng', 'st*o*nes', 'p*oo*l' and 'n*o*te'. Words are linked alliteratively, like '*th*ickly' with '*th*ere' or through assonance, like 'th*i*ckly' with 'b*i*ckerings' and 'st*i*ll'. On each occasion the stresses, created through this lineation, underscore the complex phonological design.

The use of alliteration was always important to Jackson in his poetry. In his very early writing he developed a whole symbolic schema for the visual 'notes', the letters, he used. Each letter had its own philosophical and mystical resonance, almost like the Anglo-Saxon runes used by the early alliterative poets. Jackson later largely abandoned this system, but the vestiges of such a complex idea were still carried over into his later work. In the extract above, the key alliterative sounds are 'b', 'l' and 'o'. In Jackson's system, 'b' represented both giving and blossoming, 'l' represented the spring and smoothness, and 'o' was the door into the divine; all ideas which could be applied to the transcendental sound of the nightingale singing.

When asked the question, 'why do you write such short lines?' by his friend the poet A.S.J. Tessimond, Jackson's reply provides another helpful analogy. 'The rhythm is one of a whole succession of lines, a rhythm like sea waves or something; and the line-stresses throw up the meaning in an exact and pointed way absolutely necessary to what I have to say and obtain a result unobtainable otherwise.' [18]

The analogy of the sea is an exact and expedient way for the reader to envisage the culminative and hypnotic effect of Jackson's lineation over the length of his long poems. This is exemplified in poems such as *Time Suspended in Equatorial Africa* and *Abidjan*, when he describes the sea or in poems such as 'First Love Making' when the sea is an aptly chosen metaphor to conjure up the rhythms of love making. In *Abidjan* the lineation provides a fluidity and movement that synthesises the rhythm of the waves and the breath of the reading voice, unifying form and content, the reader and the speaking voice.

> [...]The pounding, the
> Repetition and dissolving
> Obliteration of the water
> (By which all is
> Turned to
> Smoothness, movement,
> To a sliding
> Remodelling of the sea's
> Stuff and
> The sand) dissolves
>
> Thought, awareness, memory,

Within me; so that I
Become, within,
One
Vastness – one blank – one
Magnificence, the forms
Of which, changing in each
Particular, are not
Fixed, ever, for
A moment. I am

Loosened, loosed, relaxed
Entirely – by being
Made all
Movement.

Similarly, in *Time Suspended in Equatorial Africa*, the portrayal of the sea provides the perfect analogy for the ever changing lineation and rhythm of the poetry: 'the sea / Is different / Every / Moment: each wilting / And each / Budding wave is / Different – altered by / the wave before, the shore, and/ Perhaps by / Currents further out. /.../ The movement takes the / Place of / Thought, of feeling / Being.' The lines of Jackson's verse are continually modulated by the previous rhythm, 'budding' and 'wilting', with the stress pattern, as the syntax opens and closes. The stresses behaving like the drumbeats he so accurately recaptures in *Abidjan*.

The musicians went
On, on – playing
Over and over again, with
Just the slightest
Variation, the same
Phrase, long drawn
Out, complex; which got
Gradually into your
Blood, your bones, working
Up till
You felt

Exaltation – and an
Admiration for
The minute
Mathematics of the
Passage: which changed
Hardly at all, but

Changed; and
Changing yet
Again, and
Again,
Repeated, made
Its effect.[19]

This poetry has the same effect on the reader who allows the rhythm of the lines into their 'blood and bones'. As the passage from *Spring Beneath the Alps* revealed, there is a 'minute mathematics' of complex phonological and visual phrases at work in these poems that, though hardly changing, are nevertheless changing and making their effect again and again through repetition. Persist beyond the initial technical unfamiliarity of the writing, and the enchantment of the sea or the entrancement of the drum reveals the vision.

When readers have familiarised themselves with this way of reading, the message of the poems is clear. The diction is simple and largely unmetaphorical. To use the words of A.S.J. Tessimond, the writing has a 'cleanness' about it; uncluttered by either a persona or a 'free-floating lyrical I', the whole aim of his style is to make things clear. Jackson's words, descriptive rather than metaphorical, act as a clear lens to reveal the world, 'the point',[20] the meaning of existence that he sees everywhere about him, 'clear as a glass of water'.[21]

Images and descriptions are repeated throughout the long poems like a recurring melody or refrain, or fill a shorter lyric. Images from the natural world are Jackson's favourites. As Edmund Blunden wrote to him in 1942, 'your sense of Nature is choice in the detail. I think John Clare would have said so.'[22] And one image occurring regularly in the poems is that of the dewdrop, shining in the early morning sun with heaven's light. His poems are hung with a 'dew jewellery'.[23] It is an image that reveals most succinctly the vision infusing the poetry, a revelation of the mystical, Eastern celebration of beingness and nowness that Jackson was determined to offer up to the world. The dewdrop is the 'pearl', the 'diamond',[24] the gift he so insistently wished to press into his reader's palms.

It is a gift, full of the integrity and generosity of the poet. A gift of 'a most interesting and original talent, individual to the point of eccentricity, but a vehicle for all sorts of unexpected perceptions.'[25]

It is a gift which can open doors, not just to the poetry but to the world around.

All the poems, with the exception of *Abidjan*, are commercially unpublished. Although Dawson Jackson financed the publication of twenty-four collections of his poems in soft-back volumes (under the Lilstock Press imprint), these were gifts for his friends and family and did not reach a wider audience.

Poems in this selection have been chosen from the following self-published collections: *Delhi, Parts I, II, III* (1964); *The Elder Brother* (1966); *New York* (1967); *At Fifty* (1967); *Tropical Africa Parts I, II, III* (1968); *Young Women, Part III, Ice and the Orchard* (1973); *The First Morning of the World* (1983); *Spring Beneath the Alps* (1985); *The Glass of Truth* (1990). Wherever possible I have taken the text from the master copy of these volumes.

Other poems have been selected from unpublished typed manuscripts: *Twenty Portraits* (date unknown); *Remembrance Of Venus* (1969); *Next* (date unknown); *The Wound* (1983-6); *A Marriage, Parts I, II, III* (1986); *Age: Abundance and the Exit* (1990-94).

Jackson became a compulsive reviser of his work, often returning to volumes of poems written forty or fifty years previously and redrafting their contents. Fortunately for an editor, each revision is meticulously dated and I have chosen, as far as I can be certain, the latest draft of each work.

All the volumes of poetry, the unpublished manuscripts, letters and the rest of the literary papers are to be found in the Dawson Jackson Literary Archive, as part of the Special Collections at the John Rylands University Library, Deansgate, Manchester.

Nicola Simpson

NOTES
1. Dawson Jackson, 'My Poems', unpublished prose written at Hellidon, 10 July 1936.
2. Jackson, 'First Love Making', see below, p. 111.
3. Jackson, from an unpublished collection of Apothegms, written in 1937.
4   Jackson, *Against Destruction* (London: Victor Gollancz, 1984).
5. Jackson, from an unpublished collection of poems, 'Apprenticeship Volume One'.
6. Plowman, letter to Dawson Jackson, October 1937.
7. Jackson, *A Primer of Necessary Belief* (London: Victor Gollancz, 1957).
8. Ibid.
9. Ibid.

10. Jackson, from 'Out of Step, A Diary of a Conscientious Objector, 1939-1940' (unpublished), 5 October 1939.
11. Ibid., 28 October 1939.
12. Charles Tomlinson, quoted in the blurb for *Abidjan* (Manchester: Carcanet/ Lilstock Press, 1990).
13. Walt Whitman, Introduction to *Leaves of Grass*.
14. Jackson, 'The Gift', from 'The Glass of Truth', unpublished.
15. Jackson, 'Out of Step', 28 October 1939.
16. Jackson, Miscellaneous Early Prose, unpublished.
17. Michael Schmidt, *Abidjan*, p.309.
18. Jackson, Miscellaneous Early Prose, unpublished.
19. Jackson, *Abidjan*, see below, p. 31.
20. Jackson, 'The Point', see below, p. 133.
21. Jackson, 'Glass of Water', see below, p. 149.
22. Edmund Blunden, letter to Jackson, unpublished.
23. Jackson, 'The Marriage', see below, p. 175.
24. Jackson, 'The Gift'.
25. Jackson, written under the pseudonym of Thomas Brackley, in reply to a rejection letter from the editor of Harvill Press, 16 July 1942.

Spiritual Journey

One day I shall (or perhaps it is that I have done this, and I remember and respond to it; or that I shall do something of which it is an analogy; or that I have something in me that it symbolically expresses) go out, leaving all my friends, writing and property; I shall not cast these off but make a loop of time in which they are suspended to be resumed at some further date without a break. I shall come back; no one would be tied not to change during the absence, but I should come back, at no fixed date, but surely with a definite all-integral and concrete purpose achieved, and be as I was before, but with increased wisdom.

I should cease to write during this absence and communicate little with my friends, and have little or no money. Perhaps I should go on the road, living in the open or common lodging houses, but I know this; that I must be extremely poor and without roots. I must plumb many depths.

Perhaps my meditative caverns and angelic perceptions may furnish me with paths and orders; and perhaps I may be able to speak directly from the spirit, and move from place to place and person to person when I may speak it, and this will be my sole continuity.

The object will be to love, help and organise, inspirit, and by this refine and make wise and bright my own spirit. When I feel this joy stretching out before me, I see many horizons, all opening up to me, and I passing over great distances among them. My object and necessity will be to discover; in myself and the outside, the spiritual organisation of the world, in its breadth (of distance and different kinds of men) and in its depth of poverty, both materially and spiritually.

For this journey I should have to abandon my personality, and there with all personal feelings, all interest in the universe in its touching of myself, all personal friendships and man-woman love, all home and possession, all thought of the future, all care and concern with myself. Instead I should have to project myself, entirely into the outside world and people, becoming a pure mirror of the spirit moving within them, so that everything can be a medium to me, I must be only an entity conveying a blessing and message of joy and light and wisdom.

Finally I shall be able to remove the cloak from my shoulders in one movement, and go out with the naked light – unhampered by my personality, or by my perception of other people's, or by the cloak over the light and blinding form of heaven; which shall be my strength and message.

Dawson Jackson, 2 December 1934

Apologia – literary

He approached things from a quite different direction from his contemporaries, which no doubt is the reason why publishers and reviewers did not at once take to him.

He not only struck out on a different technical path but also challenged the whole destructive, eventually suicidal, course that our culture has embarked on.

At the same time, through what was around him, the commonest things above all, for him heaven shone: a heaven in no way to be divorced from the hell which is the other side of things.

His writing is direct, clear, simple: refined down until it achieves a keen cutting edge. It is highly visual: ordinary things often being seen as if their lineaments were those of heaven above, repeated. Underlining it is an anger on behalf of the deprived in society, and other species in nature; and above all an awareness that beneath life, and stretching beyond it out through death, lies an existence that transcends it. Its material being the events and feelings of a particular person's life: his own.

Dawson Jackson, September 1992

JOURNEYS

From *Abidjan*

'Take us,' the young boys
Say (inland in
The Ivory Coast), clinging
To your car, 'take us
With you to
Abidjan!' – as one
Might say, to
Heaven. Aspiration,
Hope, the way
Ahead
Lie here.

So too
In the night clubs
Of Treichville, the local
French – and
Visiting Europeans of
All sorts, and
Sailors from the port – frequent, the
Girls, charming, charmingly
Dressed, and beautiful like so
Many of these
People, offer themselves,
Open, easy, amateur, to
Share – not just
The money – but the
Radiance, the brilliance,
That shines
Out from
The magic West.

For the West is
Magical. These transistors, concrete
Buildings, the bright cotton
Cloths of the
Dresses in the streets, oil for
People's lanterns, tins

Of milk – ships, aeroplanes – and
The town's mechanics, senior
Officials, managers, small
Industrialists, all

Materialise out of the
Blank
Sea and sky from
The unseen, unbelievable, in
Everything to be
Emulated
West. One aspires
Here to live a

Life which is
Not of
This place: and lives
Therefore – trailing
Behind – by the
Courtesy
Of France: with which one
Never can
Catch up.

From this admiration
It is easy
To progress to
Envy and
A bitter hate. The more bitter
Because what
Binds, what enslaves
One, is
Not only
Colonists, or Europeans
Even, but

Oneself: one's own
Desires' contradictions
In the position
One's been born
In. The West

4

Has won; and the world
Moves in its wake.

Has won – at the
Moment. For already
The picture
Complicates: is reshaping
Itself. Nothing in life

Moves in a
Straight line. What seems
Certain, inescapable,
Today – looks quite
Different tomorrow. Every
Day it's
A new morning.
So
Don't despair. Or feel
Secure either. All things
Bend.

At any rate it's
Good to see
That since I was here
For a few
Days
Six years
Back, there have been –
Thanks to
Independence – certain
Startling changes. Not

Merely (an ambiguous
Benefit) in
The look of the town – many
More new
Buildings, and a second
Landscape – long straight
Bridge – but

In the bearing
Of the people. They
Do not, as they did
Then, glance aside
And wait until you
Speak – but look
You level
In the eye, like free
Men, like people; and often
Call out to me
A greeting: 'Ca va?', 'Bonjour!',
'Bon jour, Monsieur!' Or
More frequently – at any
Time of day – 'Bon
Soir!' Or

'Bon soir, Papa!' In Africa
It's honour to
Be Dad.

So Independence is
Independence
After all – to an
Extent. And if
Africa is not
Independent of
Our wealth, our power, our
Glamour – neither

Are we, God,
Help us. We're
Caught, enslaved
By the
Damn thing too.

There's only one world
After all; and
You can't get
Out of it. Nobody can.
The whole creation's
In it. There's
One ring round the

Lot: a circle.
The centre of
Which is
Me, or you –
Or one of
My mosquitoes or a
Hibiscus bush – whatever
The individual door may be

One chances to have
Entered this
World by – and so
To look out from
At the rest.

*

[…] I walk along
The central
Island, stepping over tree
Roots – and aside to
Let pass young men
Coming from the
Opposite direction: or women,

Their market basket on
Their head, and
A baby, a year or two
Old it may be, held
On the hip and feeding –
As the mother
Walks on
With the other
Women – at the
Large lax
Breast (which it

Can reach
Round to
And lift up
For itself

7

Till it has that
Casual
Constant
Plaything, that key
Joy of its infant
Empire, the
All-its-life-long, familiar
Nipple
In its mouth).

An older woman,
Carrying a bucket
Of clothes, for washing, on
Her head – with a baby
On her back and two scattering
Small children
To herd – breaks
From the island's kerb and
Makes a dash
Across the road in a
Lull in
The traffic, with ungainly

Caution holding the
Level basket
Balanced
While the sleeping baby
Bounces, heavy and loose,
Against her from
Behind: her eyes,
Wary and scared – with
Reason – watching
At once the arbitrary
Cars (which she was
Not brought
Up with) in the
Distance, and
Her chickens.

*

[…] Children – round a
Mother squatting in
The evening on the
Ground before her door – suddenly
Like a shying flock take
Fright, at
The sight of the
Passing
European (seeing his
Alien eye
Upon them) and seek
Shelter
Behind her.

This gay amusement
Of the woman shows
That they must
Feel, as I
Do, relief
At the abrupt removal
Of the barricades raised,
Invisible, bewildering,
Between our two
Worlds – and the
Discovery, fleeting
But brilliant like
The flash of a wing, of
Common, level, human ground
Between us.

*

[…] A crowd of hands are
Held out, up, to
Me, round me, to be
Shaken: half a
Dozen – more. Children of
All ages, up to
Nine or ten. In
The bag over my
Shoulder (with lunch

In it, and writing
Paper) is a tin of
Soap solution,
And a stick with a
Ring at the end, for
Blowing bubbles. Sitting

On the bench, I
Extract
It: slowly, with
Difficulty – one's
Bag gets
In a muddle, and I am not
Sure at first that
Today I
Have this with
Me. (Being now

A grandfather, usually
I have – that
Or balloons, or
Something; one needs
Them; leaping at the
Chance to
Be – two
Generations later, without
Selfconsciousness – a small
Child again.) A silence

Of solidifying, intensifying
Anticipation. They pile up
Round me – on
Me – on
The bench. At last I

Have it
Out. Incomprehension. I raise
The stick:
Blow gently.
Nothing happens. Again: a few
Bubbles – they float off,

Many coloured, light
Upon the air, among the
Surrounding faces.
Admiration! And
Apprehension; soon allayed.
More. The bubbles
Drift away, high – down
The street, round the
Corner of a house. I have all
My audience's
Attention: they cry out
Like the crowd at
A football match when
Someone scores a goal. Low
Bubbles are caught
Quick – as if by
Pouncing kittens. There are

Now about twenty
Children. I feel as
Though I were in the
Middle of
A black

Ant-heap. Climbing
Out, I move round
Behind the back
Of the bench: the
Children line
Up, on
It – and here at my
Side
Of it surge
About my knees.
One go

For you – starting
With the youngest (who
Is slow) – and you, and
You; then back
To the first again. They

Can all
Do it.

The feel of those
Young puppy
Bodies all
Over me is entirely
Delightful. Delicious. And

Their absorption in
What is going
On; in the

Exhaustless
Birth and release of
Those magical, iridescent,
Ephemeral, freely
Floating bubbles, almost
Weightless, sensitive
To the finest invisible
Thread of motion
In the air.

We too have, and
Enjoy together,
Common ground; for
Which I
Am grateful.

Now I
Must get on
to work. I
Extricate myself. And a changing

Wind of interest
Scatters them once again, almost
Before I've gone.

*

One day I saw
Some of those
Same children
Playing a game
Equally absorbing: beating
(These were all
Boys) with sticks
At something
Hung on a fence. It
Was a dying
Lizard. And

Another day
In a street in the town
I passed a gay
Gang, chanting
A song as they
Marched along
In a procession. Before
Them, on two sticks,
Hobbled a
Mocked
Cripple – their
Own age.

Children
Are children. And will
Be men, women – little
Altered. Angel

And devil. So we
All are. Here
In miniature
In children is
Our adult
World: the same
World the
World over.

Yet how delightful
The feel of those
Unselfconscious

Puppy bodies
Crawling, confidently, all
Over me like a sea – the boys'

Cropped
Heads' harsh
Lamb's wool, and the
Girl's hair
Teased out into
Tufts from a scalp
Mapped out like
A chessboard, one
Tuft to each
Square!

Born, we are
Thrown naked
Among loves and
Lions. Hyenas!

*

[…] From the oblique broad
Motor road that
I first set
Out on strike
Avenues – crossed by
Smaller sandy
Side streets, like
The one I next turned
Into – into the

Thick
Of Treichville

Along one of these,
At a corner, is
The shop
Where I buy
Most of
My provisions: open all

Day, and
Half the night.
Upon the doorstep

Sits a woman, with
Small pyramids of
Limes, a few
Bananas and a
Pair perhaps of
Paw-paws, set out for
Sale beside her: a child
At her knee, and another, half
Asleep, toying with her
Wide breast.

The shop
Itself is a
Minute
Cube, solid with
Wares – tiny
Tins of milk, packets of
Soap powder, lanterns, eggs,
Bottles of beer,
Baskets, almost
Anything you could want.
The owner's wife, with their
Small children; and always
The proprietor
Himself; standing, talking to
Friends who casually drop
In, and briskly
Serving customers.

Shut, the shop
Becomes no doubt
Their home.

[…] Food in the open, at
The street side (fruit, fish
Grilling in the evening over
Braziers, and coarse plantains

And corn cobs roasted
Upon embers).

*

The mosque,
Among the crowds and cars and
Commerce (everyone in
Abidjan seems
To live by
Selling things
To someone else), presents

Cool areas
Of greyish white
Outside, mounting to
Four low
Minarets – and is
A high, great, dim
Cave of

Peace
Within. Prayer mats
And emptiness. Beside

It, encamped upon the
Pavement, are
Elderly men – the trimmed
White beard
Startling
Against the brown-black
Face – each with
His mat and
Water kettle, the rest of
His possessions being
Hung up, as though he
Meant to live there for
Some time, on
The mosque's
Outer wall. Beads

In hand, they have
Small piles of cowrie
Shells before them, and
Perhaps a few white
Skull caps
To sell. Some –

Stretched right out –
Sleep, beneath the
Legs of
The passers-by: painfully,
With the dignified uncomfortable
Pathos of the aged.

In this
New town, these
Are almost the only
Old people
That you
See: the past

And the outdated
Wisdom – the solidity,
Weight, worth – of the
Old
Of Africa are

Elsewhere: inland, where
Indigence, hunger,
Hardships
Are, and memory's
Long root – in
Those vast
Tracts, horizon

Beyond horizon and
Horizon
And horizon, of
Yet
Unaltered land.

Out beyond
Adjame the road extends
Through a broken

Countryside of
Bright green
Felled bush and patchy
Cultivation: where
Villagers thread their
Way down
Paths soon
Swallowed in the green – and

Pad along
The hard, red
Sun-baked earth of the
Road side.

Where the land
Folds down, and
The road dives
With it, suddenly a
Width of
Water, white and blue,
Appears; and

Between that
And the road lie
Washed clothes
Drying – a field of
Diverse bright
Rectangles – spread out
Upon the earth and grass.

Here, at a petrol
Filling station – where lorries,
With their unimaginably
Large loads of
Two or three
Gargantuan

Tree trunks
Stand – a
Road strikes

Off upward
To the right
Into the wall of

Solid forest which has
Closed the view on
That side since
We left the streets,
Like the breakers
Of a besieging
Sea: between

Which and the sea
Itself the town of
Abidjan, with its
Spread out
Suburbs,
Floats.

The forest, rising
Up the slope, is
Like dense
Moss: solid
Underneath and displaying,
Above, varieties

Of greens, of leaf
Forms, branch forms
And of tall trees'
Tower heights, among

Which are the neat
Loose stars
Of palms.

This is what – all
Round, on the land
Side – the town has
Pushed away; and
What will roll

Back, springing up
Again where
This city stands
Today, once the
Human life, now vigorous,
Taut within
It, weakening
Grows slack: a green

Still
Sea – wave upon high
Wave of it
Out over
Horizon and horizon – breaking

Here in
The oceanic
Breakers of an
Abrupt
Forest edge.

*

As I walk
Into it, the green
Sea (its depth
The smooth tall
Tree trunks)
Close about
Me: and I

See, not
Now the lit
Leaf surface, but (all
At once) still,

Dimmed, the
Within
Of this forest
Water world – as if
I were now
Under water.

The bright patch
Of the point at
Which I entered
On the road – like a white
Water surface – pales

And, as the road
Curves, is
Extinguished.

I am in a
Tall tunnel,
Cathedral height: in
A solidity of forest
More dense
Than the human life
Of packed
Treichville or Adjame. An

Even, stilled, cathedral
Underwater light. And
Silence. Not
An insect. Hardly the
Creak of a bird – up

High and away to
One side
At some distance. Only

Straight stems of
Great
Trees, which make
High islands
High up
In the upper air; stems

Slimmer, but as straight,
Whose leafage,
Lower down, cuts
Off one half of
The light; and,

Dense as fur, the
Stems of
Small scrub
Undergrowth, which one
Could – treading
The forest floor's
Leaf mould – scarcely
Push through.

It is as though I
Have scared the
Fish, the life,
Away. No animals: no
Animation. Myself and

Trees and trees: stems
And the underneath
Of leaves – seen mostly
Dark against
The diffused light
Filtering through
From the heights

High above
Us like
Clouds, billowing
Up toward the concealed
Sun.

The yellowish green
Gashed leaves of
Monstera deliciosa, the
Size of half
A newspaper swarm, from
Unseen beginnings, forty

Fifty feet up
The tree
Trunks, upon a
Serpent stem
That roots
Into the bark. More modest
Philodendron, mounting
Throws out
A smaller, darker
Shield-shape
Of leaf; and drops down

Into open
Areas
Of air, suspended,
Thin threads which
Feel for a
Fresh point of
Purchase (budding
At the tip) to swarm
Up from
With a new
Spring of life.

No other colour
Than these
Greens: no
Flowers at all.

Stems around me; leaves
Above, and lower
Down wherever
They can
Catch the light; with

Creeper threads (and
Threads of tree
Roots growing from
Trees' branches – exploring,
Slack like an untied
Rope) hanging
Down.

I have no
Language, no vocabulary,
To describe this
Solid, varied,
Road-pierced world
Around me; so
Shall be

About it, as
It itself
Is, dumb.

Eventually I
Swim
Back, out,
Up to the
Surface once

More of
The forest edge.

*

[...] Once, in the day time,
Outside one window the
Whole sky grew
Black, and without
Warning (I
Shut the window)

Fell. The rain
Sluiced down
From the sky, wetting
Anyone caught out
In the street, through, in
A few
Seconds. The mothers

Drew indoors, collecting
In no particular hurry
Cooking pots and

Children; and the streets
Emptied, except
Where the people sheltered, in the
Freshened air,
Under trees and
Eaves. Slim

Children strolled
Naked; and in
The beer bottle and wood yard

Men, half-stripped, washed
Themselves, busily, in the
Free showerbath
From heaven – which
Thus came to them
Without need for
A long journey with a
Bucket to the tap,
Others brought
Out hand
Basins. And the whole
Yard, as the black
Sky fell, became a
Vigorous
Bathroom – which had

Been work place, restaurant,
Dormitory, debating
Hall and games yard.

The town was
Washed through
By the welcome
Wetness from the sky: a shower of
Life – of water's
White – in the
Obliterating form
Of flood, of darkness.

Fresh – it was
Soon finished. The last
Drops
Relented. And

Streets and yards – as
The precipitating tension
Eased, and the blackness
Drew back
Above the forest – filled
Up again with people: as
They had been before the
Heavy sky's

Invasion, before this calamitously
Life-renewing, thunderous, hissing, abrupt

Revolution: which left
For some hours after
In the heat a

City of muddied
Sand, and puddles.

*

[…] Sometimes, among these streets,
I hear the
Sound of music, drums
Amplified, and – in

A backwater where
Are no dangerous
Dark forms of
Cars, bumping, too fast,
Upon the pavementless
Uneven roadway – find a

Mass of people
Blocking up the fairway,
Sitting, standing; while

Children, like starlings, are
Perched on
Window ledges, all quiet
Attention, to get
A better view.

Beyond the dark
Mass of them
Is bright light
And a space
cleared – in which are

People dancing; great
Women, in a brilliant
Cloud of cloth, moving like
Slow mountains
To the beat.

Once, it was
Men and woman, all in
Voluminous
White, dancing, each alone,
Slowly, remote,
Oblivious – as if
In a trance: like ghosts,
Or angels; arms
Raised up a
Little, the eyes
Shut; slowly

Swaying, with the whole
Body as though they
Were floating, as
The music welled up
Through them, floating
Them out
Into some
Inner bliss. Those

Were, I was told,
Christians. And that
Was all I learnt.

Again – at the street
Corner next to my
Hotel, one night,
Outside a
Single-storey house
Of two or
Three rooms
Perhaps, someone

Gave a party. There were about
Fifty women. Some
Sat on two rows of
Chairs facing
One another across
The narrow pavement, drinking
Soft drinks (the evening
Crowd in the street
Beside them was
Already dense). Between the

Rows, others were
Dancing, in a long
Line, with hardly
Space to move
A foot – shiggling, swaying,
Crying out,
Laughing – to the music
Of a radiogram
From somewhere: no doubt
In the house. The sound

Went on
For hours – all
Evening. It

Was like a
Street dance on
Victory day
In England after the last
World war. But
Here neighbourliness

Does not
Need war to
Bring it out. The pleasure
Clearly

Was immense,
Gargantuan, for
Everyone. Perhaps, since
That house, or the one
Next door (judging by
The school girls one
Saw outside
Them in the
Daytime), was
A girl's school, it

Was an old
Girls' dance.

*

But best – one weekend –
Was a dance
Across the road
From the hotel: on a
Vacant plot
Near the night
Market.

Floodlights lit up
The area; and
Standing people (children
Threading among them, underneath
One's elbow) lined, a dozen
Deep, the surrounding

House walls
And the end of the arena
Where it joined the
Already jammed
Pavement of the street.
The lights, beneath

The black of night, were
Like a tent.

Four musicians, at
One end, squatted
On the floor. Two had,

Each, a
Xylophone, some
Five feet long, whose
Broad cross slats,
Of wood, up
To a foot in
Length, gave
Out, struck, each
Its own
Graduated note. While
Two had

Drums, large
As a tub, made from a great
Gourd: slapped
With the hand
Or fingers. From
Each drum's rim
There rose flat
Horns of
Leather – vibrating – whose
Edge was threaded
With small loops,
Like beads, of
Wire; which rattled,
Jangled, bell-like,
Accompanying the drumming,
Like the rim plates
Of a
Beaten tambourine.

The musicians went
On, on – playing
Over and over again, with

Just the slightest
Variation, the same
Phrase, long drawn
Out, complex; which got
Gradually into your
Blood, your bones, working
Up till
You felt

Exaltation – and an
Admiration for
The minute
Mathematics of the
Passage: which changed
Hardly at all, but

Changed; and
Changing yet
Again, and
Again,
Repeated, made
Its effect.

*

[...] The pounding, the
Repetition and dissolving
Obliteration of the water
(By which all is
Turned to
Smoothness, movement,
To a sliding
Remodelling of the sea's
Stuff and
The sand) dissolves

Thought, awareness, memory,
Within me; so that I
Become, within,
One
Vastness – one blank – one

Magnificence, the forms
Of which, changing in each
Particular, are not
Fixed, ever, for
A moment. I am

Loosened, loosed, relaxed
Entirely – by being
Made all
Movement. And washed

Fresh: wide
As the sea, great
With this
Unpetalling of the ocean
(Whose scent is
Salt, and whose
Bursting blossom the
White foam and
The booming) as

It occupies, muscular, in
Motion, the
Whole of me.

I seem, myself,
To have been
Washed up
By the sea. Vastened
To the size of
It, I leave
Myself here, and
Take
The ocean home.

From *Time Suspended in Equatorial Africa, West and East*

ATLANTIC BREAKERS

You can feel the
Earth shake – and the air
Is full of
A white
Fine spray:

We walk toward
The soughing sound, the
Booming, where
The trees thin, and

Out – onto
The shore.

*

[…] Irregularly, the
Breakers – out of
Phase with one another but,
From time to time, all along the
Shore in one
Long line –
Break: the fullness of the
Whole Atlantic

Unfolding
On this thin long
Yellow line of
Beach.

Boom! – and
A skirt of ruffled
Ruined water, a
Foot deep, is

Pushed up
The steep
Shelving of the sand. Then
It sucks

Out, rattling, with
Precipitously accelerating
Speed, like
The hissing
Breath drawn
In again: to

Be caught
Beneath the falling
Of the next smooth
Three-quarter – wheel of
Rounding, toppling,
And down

Slamming water – whose
Rushing forward
Sliding rubble is
Part

Checked by the
First wave's by now
Diminished
Sucking out retreat.

Larger and more
Perfect the
Breakers come – till
There is one long
Altogether
Perfect one; hundreds of
Yards of white
Wall
Toppling
At once, with a
Cannon

Boom; an immense rending
Running seething
Crash – satisfactory as
Everything is that's
Immense
And complete – and a
Deeper

Riot of water's
Thrust up the
House-roof
Steepness of the beach, to
Outstrip on it all
Others there have been
In the last
Ten minutes (unless
It's broken by,
Exactly timed, the
Last large
Wave's retreat):

So powerful
Are the breakers that
They shape the
Moulded flat
Sand – sculpture
Of the shore; which becomes
With each wave
A little

Different – and from
One week
To the next, thus,
Altogether altered.
The shore's
Gouged out by
The ruined wave's

Thrust forward, and
Sucked away – as loosened
Sand, to be

Deposited elsewhere.
So the

Shore alters,
Slowly,

While the sea
Is different
Every
Moment: each wilting

And each
Budding wave is
Different – altered by
The wave before, the shore, and
Perhaps by
Currents further out.
One could watch

All day.
The movement takes the
Place of
Thought, of feeling,
Being. So

The waves
Undo us, strand
By strand: as we lie

Suspended, before the wide
Sea's blank.

From *Tropical Africa*
A Notebook Kept at the Time of Independence

NIGERIA

The Sahara washed
Some of the Arab
Middle East, Mohammedan – known to
Us – to this its Savanna
Southern shore. But no one

Has yet discovered more
Than a few surface centuries
Of the history of the
Negroes and equatorial Africa
On southwards; where the sun

Stands vertical in
The violence of the midday and the earth's globe
Is at its ripe
Latitudinal extreme.

Beneath, the vegetation
Thickens
To a mass: starred with
Formal palms: unbroken, except

By villages (larger here, buff-coloured –
Packed shapelessly together
In the drowning green) of bigger,
Rectangular, mud-wall houses – and by

The gleam of the
Looping Niger,
As it enlarges: broad
Enough to push the trees apart. There

My grandfather – whom I
Last saw when
I was six – was, once,
In the early years of European
Penetration into West Africa's
Interior, almost
A century ago: liberal, Christian,
Commercial, making that graft

Which, for good or ill, is
Bearing its fruits now.

I should like to know just
What it was he was
Up to. But my family's history
Is as obscure

As Africa's; and only one
Pamphlet, on the oil-palm rivers of
West Africa – together
With some Niger Sculpture (hacked about
In the Liverpool suburb that extends
Like obliterating rain forest between
That period
And mine) – survives
To speak of him, in his vigour,
Whom I knew

In amiable bedroom slippers, white imperial,
Gold pince-nez and a
Skullcap. I just know that

He was there, whom I
Just knew: which ties, tenuously, two
Remote things
Together – and am glad
Somehow
That he was.

*

[…] The landscape
Opens out, into a huge

African city; of
A quarter of a million people –
With hardly a
European in it.
Ibadan. It is

A heaving
Sea of houses, on low
Undulating hills. Square
Mud–walls, red brown; and
Sheet-iron roofs, a rusted
Silver. Our driver

Tries, by asking passers-by,
To find his way through a
Market: stalls, shacks
People. Children, goats. The

Goats are small
And squareish: like
Kids. Well nourished. As the
People are (unlike in civilised
Emaciated India): even

Their goats
Are fat!

The road branches once
Again, out into
The country; and beneath the damp

Low sky – in the germinative
Grey, almost
English light, we swing
Onto a

Campus
Of green lawns; grown, somehow,

Here on the equator. There,
Among yellow and red
Flamboyants, that drop
Their foot-long pods,
Is spread out
Over a mile or so

A university: halls, churches,
Colleges, in the best style of
Post-war English
Architecture we see all too
Little of at home, adapted –
With open passage-ways, verandas,
Lattice walls and open Louvres – to
This climate: white, light,
Gay and peaceful,
Spaced about the green. A new

University, in
Our tradition, of our
Best buildings, written out
Airily in concrete – motorcars rolling
Everywhere about it and aeroplanes
Dropping from the sky – upon

This blank

Beginning: upon
The humus of
Mud-house Africa, which till now
Had not known
Wheel or
Harnessed animal, and whose

Perishable history – reabsorbed
Like a mud-house into
Darkness and the bush – exists

But in the present, but in
These faces (dark
Above cool robes – or European

Shirt and trousers) which
Welcome us
At a

Residential college entrance. 'Welcome',
Shaking hands, 'to Queen
Elizabeth College!'
We are shown
Along tiered verandas
To our numbered rooms – our quiet
Companionable
Cubicles. I'd like

To be a student here.

And I'd be
Lucky if, African,
I were one: these thousand
Students, now on their
Vacation, will make independent
Twentieth-century West
Nigeria, for better
Or for worse, what

It will be. That, like
The past of Africa, is stored
Away still, secret,
From us; and will be full – of
This at least one may be
Quite sure –
Of surprises.

*

[…] Printed everywhere,
By day, are
Lizards – West Africa's

Signature: written
Like lightning, and
Immediately
Still. They are

Scrawled – stamped – ubiquitously
Haphazard on the lawn
Before the College and the
White wall
That ends it: where several

Are superimposed one
Upon the other; arrested
At every
Unlikely angle, like the
Hands of a stopped
Clock. These

Take the place of,
With us, house
Mice – thrushes, sparrows. More

Than a foot long
With the tail, grey
Blue – an orange patch
At the throat and
Half way to
The tail tip – the males
Tyrannise the others: and each
Other
If they can. They rush,

Check: raise quick the
Head and shoulders; then
Flatten to the ground – suggesting
With the red throat
Something from a nightmare,
Phallic. Grey-green,

Almost transparent, their young and
The female
Are jewel-like
Sharp and fine. As soon as

Rain is over they
Put out on the lawn, just like
Attentive
Thrushes; or appear,
Dry and sudden, out of nowhere – as
If they always had been there – to make
Their mathematic statement
On the wall. And they come

Up rat-tailed – advancing
And retreating, each time a
Little nearer – to take
Scraps from outside the kitchen
(A dry-jawed
Mouthful; head up:
Listen). At your

Approach, quicksilver, they
Flow away – like
Suddenly checking
Streams of water – over
Any impediment, angle
Incline: leap
Even, with a dry rustle,

Squirrel-like,
Up the safety of a tree.

*

[…] Sitting on that
Veranda – I watch,

In the long, uncut grass
Below me, the yellow and black
Great butterflies wheel
Along like greyhounds; check
On a plant, so that I have
Almost their wing-markings
In focus; wheel on:
Return. Along

The nearby roadway pass
Women, children: an occasional
Labourer, carrying his
Heavy hoe, in
An old straw hat ... The women bear

A half gourd on the head – with various
Baskets heaped up
In it, high
With groceries – and a
Baby or young child (a lolling
Bundle of
Limp flesh) on
The back: low down,

Spread-eagled at
The spine-base. Head
On one side – it looks
Upward
Out. A child needs,

They say, to be against the
Warmth of the mother's body
Till it's a few years old: and the
 Easy
Amiability of the
Adults, reared thus, suggests
They might be right. These head

Weights the women
Carry – to support
An unmechanised
Economy, which
Pins them in their place – give

Them a slow, upright
Rhythmic
Dignity: so calm, so beautiful.

44

To rest a moment
At the roadside, a woman
Raises both arms
To the head-load and
Lifts the whole weight
Off; lowers
It, carefully kept level,
To the ground; then,
Sitting, unwraps the

Cloth the child is
Held in – from where it is tucked
In, flattening, above the
Spread, wide
Softness of the breasts – and slings round,

With one arm, the clinging bundle
To her knee. All this
Uncovered flesh, of the women
As they sit – or pace

Past
Burdened (its sensuousness
Accentuated then
By the limp
Inertness of
Their baby – with its black eyes
Rolling up
Towards you, and long, lolling
Head) – takes at
First a
Little getting used to

*

I just found time,
Between work and rainstorms. To
Walk out of the campus and
Spend an hour or so, without car
Or companions,
In the bush:

As one might swim
Naked out to sea. Wearing,

At work, thin cotton only
And free sandals – I had nothing
To protect my skin from bites
Of unimagined insects except the

Official's clothes I had
Brought with me for parties
With this country's ministers and for
Sitting in committees. So

I set out
In full formal dress –
To enter the nearest that
I was to know to
Bush: shoes, two
Pairs of thin socks (against
The sandflies); thick
Carefully creased trousers; a jacket;
And tie, to close the
Opening at the neck. And my
Umbrella; the sky was

Heavy, low,
Impending. (Between
The trees, that afternoon, there showed
Hardly one
Opening of sun.) In addition,

Spoiling the effect
Somewhat, I
Tucked my wrapped-round trouser ends
Into the top of my outer
Pair of socks, to close
The upward opening, and
Keep them out of mud: the way one does

To escape pricking, when –
Caught without bed in the English countryside –

One sleeps
Inserted in the warm peace
Of a haystack.[…]

The path
Leads
In – to a close
Unending world: as if one were within
The flesh of some
Other creature's body.

Yet, in this
Solidity, appears
Another world, subaqueous,

Like an apparition:
Submerged spaces, netted in –
A loose, diffuse
Cellular formation. Look

With one eye, and the forest is
Continuous; punctuating palms, great
Timber trees, undergrowth
And creeper – dense,
Packed together, like a rich
Christmas pudding. Look with

The other, and
Before you is a patchwork
Of carefully
Cultivated fields, tall trees
Above them: maize,
Groundnuts, occasional
Banana, pineapple, low groves
Of coca – and various
Crops I can't identify: a thorny

Thin plant six foot high, and others
Including, I think, though
I should not recognise it,
Coffee. The entire

Flesh of the forest has
This cellular network
Projected
Upon it; is hollowed out with
Holdings, peasant fields – like
The field patchwork of
The English countryside – by
Hand: the produce of
Which is
Carried, barefoot, on the head down
Narrow beaten pathways. A network

Scratched in, vaguely; ephemeral,
Like a vision
You could almost flick away.[…]

*

GHANA

Cars: yellow, tooting
Taxis. Small factories, shut now
For the siesta: workmen are
Sitting on their steps – eating lunch
Out of tin basins, drinking from old beer bottles, and

Reading papers which give just
Ghanaian, and some African,
News. Piles of

Dust and rubble; two miniature
Cocks, fighting (goats
Are prohibited
Inside Accra). Tables along the
Street-side at
Which women sell single
Cigarettes, charcoal, candles, and

Plantains grilling over an old
Enamel basin full of embers. Before them

48

Runs an open concrete
Drain, that collects waste water

Through runnels from the houses and
The alleys just behind. Where it

Is wide, crossed by a plank, it could
Engulf you – at
Night, in the half-light.

There is a bench out on
This street, in front of the hotel, beneath four
Palm trees: upon which

Guests, such as myself,
And passer-by may sit
To pass midday –

Or the quiet evening, when sounds
Even of the invading horns of taxis
Fall away, and a soft clear sky is left,
Tinged with the remains of sunset

And then illuminated by high
Diffuse stars
Or the moon.[…]

*

Often, in the evenings, I
Sit in a bar and drink
A *Fanta*. These bars
Are scattered
Everywhere among the
Small streets: in little
Concrete buildings – or in wood
Or corrugated-iron
Shacks, floored roughly
With concrete. There are old

Grimy easy chairs, forms, or
Battered iron
'Modern' chairs made
Of piping: lattices or
Windows – open – through
Which the air
Fans: sometimes
Even, to be used
In summer, an
Electric fan.

Their customers
Are the African
Middle class: people such as,
If travelling, might
Stay at my hotel. No
Europeans.
King's Bar, Easy Bar, Week-End
Californian Chop Bar, Patience Store Chop
Bar, Freedom Canteen,
Papa Joe's Café. The

Chop bars
Are rough: food is cut up,
Pounded, and
Stewed in an open pot
Outside, on the pavement,
In the dust; while, within,
One eats on a form, on one's knee
Without a table, from a chipped
Enamel basin, with
The fingers. The rest, for

The most part, serve
Drinks
Only: soft drinks: the usual
Expensive Dutch beer, and beer
Brewed in Accra. Ease,

Conversation, a
Cracked radio: occasionally
Dancing. [...]

One particular bar
Became my pub – across the road
From the hotel: managed by a
Young Togoan (out of work – the owner
Was his uncle). Two boys,

Twins, of seven, in
The evening – clad
In torn cotton singlets, and
Trousers that just
Stay up – are learning (each
On his own slate: kept,
With great care, in a satchel) the
Six times table. One of them
Lies on a couch, looking
Up at the company, absent,
Muttering; while the other
Copies out his exercises
In chalk on the
Rim of a wooden
Chair back. Beside the counter

A woman sits, sewing and
Attending to
Her baby (its sponge,
Nappies and a chamber pot,
Kept in a pink
Plastic
Bucket – which she carries about
With her
Like a handbag). Her daughter – of

Perhaps four, in a dress frilled
At the neck and
Silver earrings – makes
Delightful love to me; leans back, small
Body between my legs, and
Smiles wide for kisses: mocks
At my beard and
Melts into my flesh.

KENYA – NAIROBI GAME PARK

The thirty-five mile
Wild tract
Of the Game Park (on the
Town side partially
Fenced in: living
Alongside it, you may find

An ostrich
In your garden – or lose that
Delicacy, your dog, to
A lion, if
You leave him out at night) is

Entered in the sealed
Capsule of a car – which, hard-backed
Like a beetle, might have been
Designed
Expressly for the purpose. Baboons

Stalk, dog-like – proud,
In their short dignified
Cape-jacket like
A mane. Encountered (one
Drives slowly) they

Sit on the bonnet – straight
Nose topped by two
Brown eyes close together – and
Look quietly in
To the closed car's
Fish-tank, demanding, as though
They were English eighteenth-century
Footpads,

Bananas; which one puts into
The finger-nailed black
Human hand
Through a crack at the top of the window. They

Climb then along the almost
Creviceless smooth sides,
Leaving earthy footmarks: signature,
When one gets home, of
The day that's ended.

A dry grass plain
Of thin thorn scrub and
Tree-filled gullies
Floods
The horizons: dotted

With animals – as densely
As our home
Dairy land
With cattle. Grey

Gnu. Impala –
Cinnamon, their twisting horns
Upright. Hartebeest, bearing high an
Elaborate
Forehead-and-horn erection above
A sad, long nose. And Zebra,

Which – but for the bold
Awning-stripes
Of black and white that
Pattern them all over (worked out to
The furthest, most delicately unnecessary
Small detail) – might be
Large, familiar
Plump round ponies.

Each species herds
Together: in groups
Which merge – more or less
Loosely – with the rest.

Beautiful as
The finest, last
Perceptibility of

Light, gazelles are
Multitudinous
As shrimps in shallows:
Transparent, leap (a
Black band, upon
White, smudged upward
On the flank) – light – like

Fleas in the grass, like
Laughter. Dig-dig – half

As big – adult, seem the
Small
Calf of a gazelle,
Drawn with a finer pencil.

A giraffe (preposterously
Assembled: one oblique line
From the vestigial horns,
Like palpi, to the short
Tail-whisk – a dappled
Ladder)

Steps across a
Space of open grass – tree tall –
Like a lovely
Emaciated woman, as though a

Gracious, slow
Wind
Blew in its bones; stoops
To browse on a bush-top
Child-height below it. And, on the

Sky-line of a rise, the
Heads of others – if you look
Carefully – are seen
Against the afternoon
Intensifying sunlight: algebraic signs

Of some indecipherable
Significance or other, upon a periscopic

54

Stalk of neck
Like that of a
Sea-serpent. Benignant,

Gentle, enquiring: tall mild
Towers, withdrawn
Into their height.

Ostriches – their
Feather-boat
Of a body small
On man-high
Chicken legs – bend down,
Then up, the graceful
Independent
Serpent of their neck: pace,
Interestedly, forward, pecking
At the grass. Then stride

Away – head up surveying
The distance – like
A masted boat, buoyant,
Treading high
Upon feet which are almost
All one
Solitary great toe. A female

Flaps her loose, brown-grey,
Ineffectual wing (a
Boneless
Feather boa) skittishly
At dark
Male
following behind, over the dwarfed
Horizon; and they

Make off – an observation in
Another language, from another
Era, inexplicably
Uttered
In this landscape.

There, a pair of
Hyenas – leopard-spotted, large
Kohl-eyed – just revealed
Above the thinning
Mist of grass, sit,
Looking a little
Hurt and surly, sunning themselves
In an agreeable clearing
Hallowed out among the short
Sparse scrub. And,

In a gully,
Umbrella trees (bare spokes
Below; above – flat as a
Rectory lawn) bear

Baboons, sitting
On the surface as if
It were solid; while, beneath, stride
Others of the pack, shouldering forward
With stiffly straight forelegs, and picking
In the grass: ancient babies

Pick-a-back on the
Backs – short fur thatched –
Of the mothers.

Three yards from the quiet, arrested
Bonnet of our car, where
A dry stream has
Left one
Waterhole, a

Pair of lionesses – in a lazy bed of grass
Shaded by low

Comfortable scrub – lie,
Taking their all-day-long
Siesta: licking their
Round-eared cubs – ruffians,
Half-grown – who roll

Back on their backs and play, making
A game of it, paws
Upward. They

Rise, loose pawed,
Loose backed; flow, quiet,
Deliberately
Slow, toward
The hole: and drink – the
Mothers, then the six
Cubs, irregularly
Following: so that

Nothing of the hole, for
The surrounding
Lowered heads, the silent
Careful lapping
Fur, is seen.

It is lazy
Life that
Lions lead:
Who have nothing else to do
But choose, at evening, from the calm flocks
Round, whatever prey – like
Fruit upon a
Laden tree – the whim takes them
To take
That day.

Not far from this
Felinity,
Which melts like a love's
Rage through the mist
Of grass, the thin

Medieval scarecrow
Of a Masai herdsman, raises tattered
Hat on head to us, in greeting, as
We pass: pasturing

His lean herd – kept compact,
Close together – a small spear in his hand. They say

That Masai and
Lions smell each other – and keep,
Wisely, out of
One another's way. Our

Car drives us on
Home (as if we were
A returning
Submarine expedition – separated

From this other calm
Wild world, from
Africa and
Africans, by
Tin and glass, like
A crustacean's
Insulating shell) to the

Suburban
European lawn, to tea,
In equatorial bright
Sunlight (the heat cooling

Toward evening, and
The sudden
Night – violent, violet-blue
And starry): to

Peach trees, frangipani,
Roses.

From *Delhi*

A PINCH OF DUST

Dust. The cows are freer here. And

I am loose,
Exposed – trying not to look
As though I had no other object
Than to look … Buildings
Half demolished –
By time and poverty, not
Bombs. Enchanting

Half-naked children: the boys'
And babies' eyes rimmed black
Round with
Kohl. The beauty

Of these people – dignity!

And their variety: full beard
And long Sikh hair tied
Up beneath the turban; cropped
Black head, sometimes with a small
Spouting tail behind, the face
Clean-shaven; and Mongoloid
Faces from the mountains – Nepal,
Assam; or wide,
Flat, from Tibet. What grace

Of carriage! Conferred
In part by open sandal, flow
Of uncut
Cloth, and
The heaven-bearing calm
That's born of pacing
With a burden on the head – and in part
By something not to be
So easily
Indicated: inward. At any rate

We ourselves have lost it.

The dignity has
No harshness: is quick, responsive,
Warm – upon a reserved
Hinterland of all that ancestrally the

People differ from me in (which –
Though I sense what lies within
It, in the dark – I shall not penetrate
On this short visit: or
I think
At all).

Why then is it
That I feel at home

Here in the street in Azad Market? Not

Because of what England's left behind: which
Hinders more than helps –
Apart from the convenience of language (these
Knotty Englishes). It is as if

I had by travelling exposed
Something already in me. Hindus
Might say I
Had lived here before:
I don't know about that. But
In the place's unfamiliarities
I seem to be returning
To the known, familiar,
With the bright eye of absence. No doubt

The friendly welcome given to a stranger
Helps. But this
Again, is something
Familiar already to me, natural – although not
Known in England: now anew
Regained.

And why is
This India not remotely like
Anything anybody told me – not
Writers, nor relatives
Who have spent a lifetime here?
Never did book or word
Bring the place to me. Where can
Those eye-witnesses
Have been? The point

That they omitted is
That here is here. Pick up

A pinch of dust:
This is the place.

*

[…] How narrow,

How provincial, are the
Confines of one's skin! Within them
Repeating, hypnotic,
The half-deceits of your own
Point of view – you persuade yourself
The universe has no other centre
Than your own: and that conviction
Hardens until either
You must be broken
Or the world. Ah yes! All

You say holds
Water, or seems to. But listen
For the love of Christ – of Buddha, Krishna –
To the million other tongues
And languages in this vast
World outside: to other

Men, the young, old, children,
Women – other races,
Species, places,
Epochs. Nothing can make you
If you do not want to,

Except pain, and death.
They crack your shell.

*

EXPOSED

Europeans,
For some reason, do not
As a rule
Ride bicycles – travel

In public buses, or
Go third class on trains. They seem to want

To be as far as possible
Away from India
While they're there: the car
Or taxi window is
Safe, like a television screen. '*Look –*

A man with a python! … An elephant! …
Did you see, that
Man we just passed
Was handcuffed, to two others!' They turn round
And stare out of the window.
Wonderful! … Lost is all

Sense of reality, as one turns
Over the pages of the coloured magazine
Called India. Thrilling. They close it
Even
Genuinely moved.

But that felon is real –
As you are! His shame stabs
Sharp through the
Shamed
And quick-averted sympathetic eye.

Real as yourself is that
Tail-less sparrow there
Outside the window in
Your garden – living
Its keen tail-less life
In the fresh morning,
Nipping your crocuses. Close to us

In His complete love, may God
See us
As what we are – as
Real: from
Within. I

Then, on the contrary,
Enjoy
A bicycle (it
Engages one, direct
With the rest
Upon the road: and, discarded,
Drops off like a sepal –
So that we all blossom
Together, open:
Undefended on our feet); and the

Sociable
Bus, in which the young Hindu
Teacher slipped, curious, into
Conversation with me: and third-class
Carriages, where one is packed

Close as in a packet of
Pressed dates with a
Cross-section of all India, their
Cooking pots, locked boxes and
Bed rolls. It is not

That I want, inquisitive,
To understand
This other life, innumerable
Round me – but to be

There,
Among it, in it: close as
Skin, senses and
A bicycle's transparence
Will bring me;

As one would smell a rose.

For, rather than in reincarnation,
I believe
In the simultaneous
Incarnation of each of us
In all. Intimation
Of which is
Given us
By love. If I am not

Now
That felon – the sparrow – there, that
Squirrel in the grass – it is

My fault
For locking myself up in
This shut self-box. Let us at
Least, thus travelling
Exposed, lift up the
Lid
A little: breathe
Something
Of that other brother life.

I,
Beautiful and light, quick gather crumbs
By the sweet stall; and
Shaven headed am hustled
Through the crowd to prison: glimpses
I just catch of
Myself, as in a street
Mirror, passing – and (were
I muffled up in my defences)
Might not recognise.

*

TEMPLE AND SHRINE

One afternoon I
Set out
For the Kutub Minar. Its

Base is – I
Had learnt – heavy,
Sculptural, twelfth-century
Hindu. And to that
Later Mughals added, scrawling
The flat decoration of their script
Down also over the wide
Ambitious
Bole. It is a single

Tower or pillar (hollow
Within – a spiral
Stair case between the core
And shell) of pink
Iron–hard sandstone; and
Rises like a
Telescope, pulled out
In successive storeys
Upward to its
Surveying summit; an open

Gallery running
Around it at each
Storey-change – at which
The style of architecture, and the
Period, change too.

*

[…] I
Got lost. The landscape became

A vague endless
Suburb – with a tomb, stripped
Grey and ghost-like to

The bone, rising
At intervals
From another era. Low

Cream-white houses,
Flat, of one
And two storeys, bear
Advertisements for
Montessori schools, grammar
Schools, evening schools – scrawled on them
In pitch. In the low-walled

Back yards are
Waterbuffalo: broad-backed
And black. The area

Has run out of English; there is no
One who can speak it, to
Put me on my way. And yet
Although the
Place is thus
Altogether Indian – treeless,

Pointless, the suburban
Atmosphere is desolately the same
As in any other such
Dead dormitory on earth. The people
Who live
Here seem content enough. I, I only

Want to get away.

*

Clear country now, or a ruinous
Semblance of it – and no

Kutub Minar: the horizon somehow
Has swept it out of sight. Slight

Irregularities of
Stony land. Tombs
About which bits
Of village cluster. Few
Trees (an isolated
Palm); thin
Dusty grass. Goats appear from nowhere:

The road bends suddenly. Women
Before me are using the road surface
For a threshing floor (behind a
Tall falling wall, a village –
Cavernous – is glimpsed), while slow
Upon them advances a rush-
Laden bullock cart. And

On the right, in a fresh
Green grove of trees, like
The explosion of a blue jay
Bursting on the sight, appears
A temple. (The first I've
Come upon: apart
From the small shrines
With which the place is peppered – and
Those stones, hardly carved, in
Fields, smeared
With the holy red.) There is

No dome
Or spire of tower; a
Fruit-like form, a wide
Four-faced
Fir-cone, erect; down which

Creep plaster tigers moulded
On a wire core, the tails
Curling
Forward down their backs. In niches, high,

Are cross-legged
Contemplatives; monkeys,
Carved; a central pair

Of heavenly lovers. And, across the base,
A row of skirted
Warriors with
Thin smiling moustaches. The whole is
Painted
Biscuit-colour, red
Ochre, brilliant blue.
A porch, supported
By blue elephants, hidden
In the grove.

*

[...] The large Sikh – cross-legged
Upon his platform, hair
Caught up with an untidy comb
Into a single knot – reaches
With flat back
Easily about his shop. Before him

Is a brazier – bearing an iron
Shallow dish of
Slowly heated milk,
Which dries
To solid curd. When cold, this

Is taken out and sold by ounces
In a cupped brown leaf – for eating
In the fingers. Meanwhile

The milk is ladled, hot, with
A small iron measure on an elongated
Rod, into
Our thick glasses – into which
A boy pours then
Boiling water from the kettle
On a second brazier, through
A sieve of sopping
Tea dust: a fresh pinch
Added for
Each glass. The dark

Brown steam pours through. Sugar
Knee deep – and the whole is stirred
Up with a spoon, vigorously,
Like a cocktail. It

Puts back, into me, the
Peace and energy
Expended on the ride; and the world
Returns to
Quiet focus. Someone has

Made room for me
On a bench. My bicycle stands
Propped up, a few yards off
Beyond a tobacco–stall. Above

Us spreads the
Light foliage
Of a mimosa
Not yet in flower. And across the road

The white domes,
Mosque–like, of a late–dated
Tomb are seen –
Opulent and elegant as if
In an Arabian tale –
Through dense shade.
Shedding trees. Peace. I am given
Even unnecessarily
Much space
Upon the courteous bench.

*

A beggar woman, whom I
Passed a mile back –

Small and perfect
In her middle age,
As though by poverty
Reduced to a diminished scale (her clothes

69

Black and thin, like the skin
Stretched over the small-boy bones) – walking
With a staff comes

Muttering up, in long
Self-communion; and begs
With uninsistent hand. The fruit-seller
Whose shop
Is balanced on a standing
Bicycle, gives
Fruit. As a matter of course
One customer
Hands a few pice – joining
Hands, prayer-fashion,
With incline of head. Another
Pushed across his saucer
Of small fritters: half of
Which she eats – sitting
Across the table from me,
Shrivelled up – and half
Puts in a cotton
Breast pocket, hot. Then she shuffles off
In barefoot solitary
Haste, alone –
At home in this society

Which has room for beggars, as
For foreigners. Outside the

Railway stations and in public
Places where the tourists are,
Begging however is
an altogether different matter; children,
Women, cripples
Pester, pestilential – horrifying
Like a cloud of flies
Not to be shaken off: lose all
Humanity. And

You, your pity raped,
Lose yours.

*

I take
A second glass and sit
On the low wall
A few yards off, smoking
A *biri*. The public tap
Pours out its water
Over a young man – who
Bathes himself, squatting, in it
Head to foot. By the overflow
A girl who might be nursing dolls
Pounds clothes from a slab
That forms part of the pavement; contentedly,
With her companion. Throws down
The wet grey mass,
Hits it with a baton, turns
It again – a little
Greyish water squeezing out – rinses,
Pounds once more. The café

Boy comes up and
Washes our used glasses. Opposite,

An old man is singing
Something to himself, asleep –
Apparently – upon
A string bed in a patch of shade: passing
His easy afternoon.

*

[...] When I reached at length
The Kutub Minar

It was late in an
Afternoon. Gold
And brilliant green. Formal

Irrigated gardens surround
The attendant ruins – which
Like an open library provide
As many diving-boards as you could wish
Into the off-shore deeps

71

Of this land's
Oceanic history. Upon the grass

In a saffron robe
Sat a Tibetan monk, come up – like
Many more – for the twenty-fifth
Centenary of the Lord
Buddha; and round
Him squatting in the shade
Were a ring of curious
Welcoming Indians.

[…] From the Minar pour
A family of
Tibetan pilgrims – in raw yellow,
Orange, and half-height
Hide boots – the upper clothes
Thrown back in the mild
Trans-Himalayan
Air: a ten-year-old

Boy, leaping and laughing
With the excitement of it,
Before them. Among the

Indian men's sheer
White – and the smooth, sharp
Colours of the water – like
Silk saris – their dry
Red and yellow strike
A puritan
Rough note: harsh; restrained – rather
Antique than
Primitive – refreshing. Two

Young monks play ball with some
Small Indian children … So

The eye rises
To the Minar. How Hindu

Is, indeed, the pleated
Sculptural irregularity, the wide
Weight, of the red
Satisfying
Base! Another
Storey, and another –
Narrowing. Above,
Yet narrower storeys –
In a whiter stone – have
Geometric
Flat motifs, of the
Mohammedans' succeeding
Book religion. Hindus
Dance – and all, for them, has
Corporeal form: dense
Gravid. While Moslems

Write out their
Floral and peak-arched patterns
Among no fertile
Jungle, but on flat
Desert sand. Theirs

Not body, but
The word; not fruit and
Heavenly lovers – but
A sword. The

Summit seems
Irregularly carved – until you see
Those are the silhouettes
Of people mounted there. Up

The inner spiral – past
Families that sit
For rest in the broad niches, which
Narrow to small
Windows (invisible from the outside,
Among
deceiving ornament). Up the

Worn, raying
Successive
Stair-treads: well–nigh
In the dark. A gallery –
Leave that, and wind up

To the top. Now,
Near evening, the tide
Of visitors flows down; one is,
Almost,
Alone. Powdery

The light plain stretches – with darker
Banks of trees, and smoke
Smudged up from villages
Unseen; on a small
Horizon are the roofs
Of Delhi. The cloudless sun

Shoots level at you
In the slightly chilling air. Below,
Intense emerald are
The park's trees in the invading
Yellow light – and over them
Swoop skimming
Backs of long-tailed green
Parakeets like

Minnows over water-weed. It is
Cool here. Cool too
Below – when I

Descend
The octaves of this panoramic
Spiral exaltation.

Dusk. Warmth, retained
In patches yet
By the kind ground. Scents. One
By one are

Undone the layers
Of light, as I stroll
Assuaged – like a flag
Un-tautened
Taken down – among
The varied levels of the
Indecipherable relics, and
The cavernous trees.

A great moon rises through the high
Neem trees, as I cycle back …

THE TAJ MAHAL

I mount the steps – each
Straight as the horizon, an
Ascent in
Gradual calm
Air – leaving

The world behind, beneath
The cloud-high trees beside the
Road, like
Stripping off a cloak. […]

I lean
Against the inner
Entrance archway; then
Ease myself into the
Garden; seen, first,
Framed
Within it.

Wide
As a pavement of the sky … No one
Had prepared
Me for
That. Green

Watered grass – beyond which
Darker trees cloak the
Terminating walls, and attendant
Sandstone buildings. While

Straight across strikes a wide water-avenue, flanked
By small erect cypresses upon
White
Figured marble.[…]

The Taj; a
Vision of
Divested
Venus. No further can
Earth be
Etherialised than this. Perfect
As Notre Dame: Persia and
India fined, together, down
To diamond. Erect,

Yet rounded
Pearl-like
Like a swan,

Calm,
Complete, pure
White – the glare
Transmuted by the
Angle of the sun – set off

By the private
Heaven-wide space – she stands

Straight at the centre.

I advance; step –
Towards this last
Light loveliness –
Out of
Myself […]

Onto her calm
Terrace, beyond
Which the river drops, I am
Caught up: her silences
Rising, resolved
About me … First, a

Sweep of sandstone terrace
Spreads its hush; thence, one
Steps up – as
Into visionary air – onto
Another; higher,
White. Upon which –

All white marble – is
Her domed
Sculpture, carved,
Out of the core of light.

All, and embracing all;
Concise, yet
Wide as the mother
Moon: it sweeps all
Up, in a still ascent to sky. […]

As the full moon
Rises we return to that other moon

The Taj. Accompanied by
A miscellaneous caravan of
Pilgrimaging India, which comes –
Each month on this
Night of the full moon – in tongas and
A rabble of other crammed conveyances

To see her white
Lit up
By whiteness
In the airless dark.

All is luminosity
And dusk. Trees

Low, are undifferentiated
Heaps of a dark
Formless substance. And, huge

As the dome, the full
Moon
Blazes: with an intimate
Intensity which quietens, abashed,
The voice – raising up
That assured calm Venus
Like a vision
(A porous, softened white),
Across her
Caverned space
Of small black cypresses, above
A weightless earth.

The air is
Barely cool – is
Free: timeless.

Beyond and below
That contained
Proportionate huge
White, the river
Disappears: curving
Without place
Beneath the lower
Broad sandstone terrace

Which extends – stretched
Out for pacing
Meditation – alive
With sight's slight
Suggestions
And faint scent.

It is late, and the ebbing
Night's tide may
Leave us stranded.

*

AGRA STATION

[...] I
Stroll onto the platform – where
The classes mix,
More or less (the strap of
One of my sandals
Flapping loose, came
Unnailed from the sole). Porters
Part-dressed in red – carrying
Tin trunks, whole
Households of
Effects, upon their heads – struggle
Shouting through the press, to get
Their patrons a
Tonga, or place. The next

Train will be mine. 'Mend

Your sandal, Sir? Eight annas.
Mend your sandal,
Eight annas!' Under
My elbow he is
Like a midge. A boy
Of about eight; carrying
A wooden box, in which is
An improvised hammer and small
Tin of tacks. A bit young
To do the job well – and not,
Particularly, cheap. No thanks. But this
Angel is not to be
Brushed off: dark,
With black-ringed
Eyes and bubbling
Amiability. 'Mend

79

Your sandal, Sir: eight
Annas.' I give him

A few annas; now
Shoo! – smiling –
Go away. It is impossible
Not to love the boy. At the far

End of the platform, the people
Thin and I find
A sort of seat. Now there are
Three boys, all with
Their boxes: 'Mend your ...'
Look, I've already
Given you something: here is
Another anna
Each: now
Be off – batting
At them gently with
My newspaper. This

Is like a game
On the seashore: the lad might
Be my son, no
Beggar. It is not just
The round beauty of his
Proportioned face – but the loving
Lively air about him. He is
As a son would be
At home. An elderly

Gentleman in a dhoti
With stern loud admonitions
And with brandished
Umbrella drives them off. Which
Is not quite what I meant. In some
Confusion of feeling, I convey
My thanks. The

Train
Steams in – and beside

Me, going
Ahead to get
Me a seat in a third
Class
Compartment (overflowing
From its windows) is, again,
The sprite. I hand him

Some bananas
I have with me and
A further coin or two – say thanks,
And goodbye. He'd
Never have got in. I
Barely can: people
Are climbing up at both sides
Through the doors and windows.

Inside, one
Sees why: the entire
Carriage – of one compartment, four
Benches running
The whole length – has two
Doors only; and is packed
Not only tight with people but
With their bed-rolls, their
Cooking pots, boxes, clothes-bundles
And even
Household furniture: leant

At one entrance are
A pair of wooden
Bed-ends. Only their
Houses seem
To have been left behind. Considerately

Squeezing up, the company
Makes a small space for me. Everyone,
Eventually, is sitting – or
Squatting – on the
Benches or the floor. Beside me

A thin old lady, almost
Devoid of substance, perches
Folded up
Like a jack-knife – knees
To chin and heels
To buttocks – occupying
No space on
The hard bench: entirely
Comfortable. Mothers
With small children, whole
Anxious families, squat quiet
Among their pots and bundles
At our feet. Above

Runs a wide luggage-rack, down the
Entire carriage – today
Piled up with monumental
Baggage only (on this
My first train-journey
At least, no one
Is stretched out there
Asleep). We wait ten

Minutes. Gradually
I become aware
Of being looked at from a window
Several yards away across the solid
Packed-in
Mass, on the off-side – the
Side onto the line. A
Small face: it is

The sprite again. He waves,
Smiles. Goodbye! Goodbye! And he goes on
Until the train moves –
Simply seeing me off.

A VANTAGE

Two exhibitions of sculpture – a
Buddhist and a Jain – are set out, in
Celebration of the twenty-fifth
Centenary of the Buddha, under wide tents
In the town. The solidity, the
Corporeal
Reality of sculpture exquisitely
Fits it to express
India; and she has made
A sculptural
High art of her own. Nevertheless

Nobody bothered to
Conserve the carvings much
Before the English, a
Short time ago. India's past

Lives on in sacred texts
Remembered, in custom, in
This moving fluent
Flesh. It is not set down
In writing. And her stone legacy was
Left to the tide of life
To the protection of
Its own hardness, not nervously
Preserved.

In the Buddhist tent,
The early sculptured
Buddha – cross-legged or
Standing – calm
Like a pool, at ease, looks
Inward

Into himself; and out
Into the calm in us and
Beyond us. In his
Gaze, contradictions – conflict –
Drown: yet no
Creature is left out. There is

In it
No hatred, even
Of evil:
No war. Only
Smooth peace. A peace part
Puritanical (like
The shallow folding of
The draperies), yet sensuous
Also: with the fruit-like weight
Of that primordial surrounding
India from which the Buddha
Was born. Peace;
And an everyday, lyrical
Humanity – such as is seen
In the paintings of the
Ajanta Buddhist caves.

This Buddha is
Humanity, without
Fault of stress. Reflected in
His, our own face
Is frightening – hardly
Civilised or sane. He

Is oneness,
All-inclusive. High – yet
Not harsh: excluding nothing. Close
To us
As dust.

From *New York*

ALIGHTED

It is like
Being dead. So wide

Deep
Is the Atlantic – which I crossed

As if in bed, in the close
Dark, attended
By a sort of staff of nurses.

It would take
Almost a divine decree – many
Weeks' salary –
To get me back again now
By a reverse wave of the wand
And return air-ticket

Over the cat's-tongue surface of
That unimagined sea, which millions
Cross but none
Seize with the imagination. I was

There
Am here
And know next to nothing about how
It happened.

Reincarnated! Every thing
Is different – and,

Like myself,
The same. New minted

This afternoon the world
Is stamped
'New York' with

Skyscrapers: nothing
That is not new
Is on it. Without

Interstice anywhere, a new life
Is packed about me. The air

Is fresh with a thousand miles of sea, and all my
History up to this moment
Is screened off
By the earth's extraordinary
Atlantic curvature
As if by the cut of a knife.
I might be dead.

And these on the pavement would be souls
Who have committed
Emigration suicide:

I, the visitor,
Keep my past
Within me to revert to,
Enriched, in four endless
Short months' time – while they,

These angelic familiarly strange
Strangers, have sunk theirs
Deep almost as the Atlantic
By a voluntary act and –
Stunned yet by the shock of it – are

American. Their lush plant
Struggles here for root
In the raw almost tilthless soil
Of a virgin
Exhilarating continent…

The air tastes good, salt – is pale,
Wide, clear.
You'd think it clean
Until you see the
Hard rock – like smuts in it,
Which pepper anything by the open window
And stops me sudden in the street
With a blow on the eyeball as
If from someone's fist. I'm

Glad I was translated.
I like everything in the place
Because it is
And is turned up bright with newness – so
Bright indeed one can hardly take in
Things so
Violently strange. People

Pass and people pass and people pass
On the pavement. Road
Intersections – the way to work's
Down there. A huge

Limousine slides
To the curb and I'm hailed
By an Asiatic delegate
From some past conference, I can't
Recall his name
Or nationality: we warmly
Greet, because
Both lost. But I'm glad

To get clear from delegates and float at large
On the pavement of America
Rigging up the first rudimentary structure
Of fresh familiarities
To house my new
Disembodied soul in. […]

ACROSS

Where shall we go?
There is the whole
Of my four months before us.

Let's keep
Just now within the city. I rarely
Stirred far out: work
Kept me on too short a string.

Stroll, say, east:
Along my Fifty-Third Street
And zig-zag
Through the Forties
Across Third Avenue, Lexington,
Park, Madison and Fifth, to
Diagonal
Broadway: at night, when that

Exaggerated thoroughfare
Is lit up
Like Piccadilly Circus but
A dozen times more so.
Theatres and cinemas jostle
One another, like the
People on the pavement: each

Holding out a heavy canopy
Upholstered over with a pile
Of lit
Lamp-bulbs. Electric
Signs are moving miracles of
Ingenuous
Ingenuity, skyscraper-scale.
Eating places. Amusements.
Saloons. A religious address
(Delivered from beneath a
Placard: WARNING!) down
A side street. And people –
Like dense moving shoals of fish

Come from the darker shallows to
This bright deep, where their
Slow steady milling
Among one another stirs up a
Ceaseless
Effervescent interest – luxuriously

Dressed, by English standards, with white,
Black, olive and
Coffee-coloured skins. Fifth

Avenue – as we return –
Is stately,
Like a glossy magazine: with
Advertisements of shop windows. There

One day I watched
A large American on the kerbstone
Take out a great cigar
And lick it carefully all over
Like a boa-constrictor before
Placing the prepared victim
In his mouth and stepping off
Into a gap between the traffic. And
Later – towards Christmas –

Wet snow fell at midday on
Unprepared perfect
Typists emerging
From high file-like offices, nakedly
Neat, yet hardy, holding

Some scrap of paper like
A leaf over
Their carefully thought hair. [...]

[...] Where shall one eat? Restaurants

Are either so dark
For the sake of intimacy
That you cannot see the food,

Or so neon brilliant
That they throw you
Transparently exposed
Out into the naked street. Try

A drug store. There
The huge hotplate
Fries impartially eggs and
Hamburgers, and an endless
Toasting belt ascends
With sliced bread – made
Apparently of air
And fluff and chalk and
Advertised exotic
Vitamins. You sit
On a stool and are served
As quick as lightning: a welcome
Glass of iced water being
Pushed across the open counter to you
As you order, to bridge
The interim. – Nowhere

Is one left time
To do more than eat
And go. No meditative
Lolling or
Conversatión, not
Even in the bars. O
For Latin cafés – the pubs
Of England – for
Time, cards, darts, peace and
Human intercourse!

Start talking
To your neighbours
If you want to; but everyone
Is moving on.

Where to?

A country boy, perhaps, will
Tell me about the small town he
Comes from, at a loss
For a friend; or a Cypriot
Café keeper will send
Messages by me to his brother
In London, whose address he cannot
Now quite remember – recall
A war
Served in some British regiment.

The friendships of the rootless
Form no tie: are
Easy, generous and –
As quick forgotten. This

City might be a ship
Of casually signed-on
Sailors; a
Sea of ships
Sailing different ways – each from
Some different
Far-buried
Half-forgotten shore. However,

Before it – clear-swept, wide
Open – lie
The horizons
Of the future!

By Grand Central Station
I sat down and wept. [...]

THE HUDSON

One weekend, I picked my way
Down through the levels of the
Rock–cut railway station and
Fitted myself
Into a train: which

Drawing out in darkness, shook
Then off the suburbs and
Slid like a serpent
For four hours
Northward
Up the curving, wide
Forest-enfolded
Hudson – a few
Millimetres
On the continental map – to

Poughkeepsie: pitched on
At random more or less, since
I wanted to pluck
The unknown
Fresh, with the dew of chance upon it.

A corridor-like, smooth
Air-conditioned train compartment:
Magazines and light refreshments
Plying along the aisle, and a

Glass wall of window
On my left. From
The twentieth century, thus
One looks out on the abiding
America, that has
Not learnt to recognise us yet.

From this spider's
Thread of railway – suspended
Light upon the land,
Now at water-level, now
High up – one sees

Hills sentient
With near naked
Late autumnal forest, folding
Wide one into another
Above the river's estuary-resembling

Space: a release to the
Imagination as though one
Caught one's breath. As

The afternoon lengthens and the round sun
Still descends, casting
At last a flood
Of yellow then quenched
Orange at us
Over the engulfing
Grey – the hills
Turn, from exact
Reality, through softening
Suggestion to
Silhouette: absorbed
By the dazzle and
Darkness of sunset. At

One point another
River joins
The sheet, and across
The silver-grey expanse
A figure paddles
A canoe: which small

Fleck
Strips the land back
To the time when it was
Comprehensible – by the Indians
Whose life, and understanding,
Took form in
Its mould. The Indians

Have been drowned out
By our European flood
From the Atlantic – and in
Their depth is lost
The only human key this
Landscape ever had. It remains
For us a raw
Incomprehensible
Enigma: painted

By painters – farmed, even –
But a few
Trivial centuries. No Turner

Or Constable has
Painted this Hudson
Light. No Chaucer
That we know, of our blood,
Has sung here
In a medieval May. No Rome
Rose here before our
Time, nor Greece
Lay round the corner. Prophets
And Christ are a whole

Unhistoried ocean off,
Beyond new-civilised Europe's
Small peninsula. What can

We do with
This noble land, but project our
Earlier life upon it –
Make Dutch and English homesteads
In temperate New England – or

Plant upon its unresisting
Vacancy a vacant
New one, created out of nothing
On the spot: the
Petrol pumps, cars, cinemas, shops and drug-stores
That run through the centre
Of Poughkeepsie, making
It the same as anywhere
In America […]

That canoe
Declared
In almost lost
Frail Indian language
The real America
That in a thousand years

Will make more mark
On us than we on it
With our ant-proud
Ingenuities.

Poughkeepsie
Has a coca-cola street
Coming in one side and without stopping
Running out the other
Into the rest of the American
Road network – which seems

To extend so steadily the same
There is no point
In travelling upon it: one stretch
Of street says all. This

Main street is, however, as
Shallow as a
Stage-set. Pierce the shiny
Advertisement-lit façade – and there,
Ten yards away, is a
Darker, quiet town

Of white-painted wooden
Houses, set
In unkempt trees and
Grass, each
With a veranda and its
Rocking chair: an architecture

Entirely delightful; more
Civilised than its English
Victorian contemporary; cool,
Formal, strict and leisurely
Like the manners
Of a century further back:
With the charm

Of authentic, earlier
America, that crisp
Cooking-apple sharp yet
Slightly vacant bracing flavour
That all the best things here have,

From skyscrapers to verse.

Around
Was scrub of sumac, wild
Michaelmas daisy in the matted
Autumn grass, thistles
I had never seen the like of, new
Spiders, insects: a

Complex formed, at
A remote time, remote
From everything I know – yet
Present, actual now

And admitting me, hard-husked in
My unadapted ignorance,
For the moment that I choose to stay. On this

High land I see
For a second, almost, over
The edge of a life-time's
Habit, into
The new world
Where I am.

From *Spring Beneath the Alps*

Each flower species, each
Finality, persists –
A pavement of heaven – a few
Weeks, days, a
Moment, and
Is surpassed
By the next.

Thus too
The light on dew
Drops
Changes – some shining
Bright, then others
Differently – as, passing

Slowly, like time's
Hand, I change the
Angle of the light: praising
The being, the birth
Of things, the morning.

You'll never stop the
Spring. And
Spring never will
Stop coming.

Is that not
Treasure enough?

[…] Never failing, spring
Yet
Cannot be recalled.

Live then in
Each season
As it comes: till, after
The full cycle

Of the year's
Changing joys, this
One, this spring which
Now slips from
You, is – fresh,
Different,
Come again.

There is one
Way however in which
You can
Recall the spring:
By walking

Uphill, into
The mountains. There

Like a memory, a
Reflection – preserved by
Altitude – of what
Was
Below, spring
Is again
Released: read back to
You again. Back

Turns the year
To what time you
Wish – and from say
The summer of
Late May you can
Mount (turning the
Wheel back
Flower by
Flower) to before
Birth: to winter,
To the snow.

There, a reservoir of
The year that's
Past is

Held: hanging, high
Up above us
In the hills – which sharpen,
Narrowing
The year (excising first
Summer then the
Spring and autumn), to
Season-less

Unchanging white.

*

[…] Here
Are tall trees, thick trunked,
Thick foliaged – beneath which,
Years back, I heard
My first
Nightingale. Nightingales

In lilac
I shall not forget.

There still is
Lilac. And coming home
One evening I could
Tell my love that
The first florets
Of the first, lowest, tower
Were open and that
That scent
Was loose

Whose wildness
She only could assuage.

[…] Nightingales sing, even
In the morning, even in the
Early evening and
At high hot
Noon: an enormous

Note, written out many
Times the size
Of that of a blackbird. First

A gusty
Lusty thirsty
Bickering and
Black chatter (there in a tree
Above me, not ten

Yards from a car
Park, and twenty
From a new building
Sprung up among these
Oaks – which have for
Generations been
These conservative bright
Birds' houses): breaking

Then out
Into the soft
Round liquid long
Sustained long repeated
Heart note, a hoot
Almost, of attained
Joy, a reiterated
Circle, O, O, O, O, soft
As smoke, round
As the placeless
Spring haze, heat haze. Then
Back to the full-throated
Clack and clatter of the
Bird's black bright
Undergrowth of song – and again, high,
The smoke ring of attained
Joy
Balances.

[…] Nightingales are
Singing – a
Wall of sound – in this
Wide open
Middle of the day.

Nightingales
Hidden in the green,
Against
Blue sky... Ah, ah – the

Violins; and
The full
Cello: O, O, O.
And bubblings, bickerings
Of black
Notes (this hedge of
Trees is a long
Line of music
Thickly scored), the splashing
Of bright deep
Water over stones; and there
Again the deep
Pool, the still
O, O, O, O again
Repeated, the deep
Full note; as when

After all our hedge
Of love making she
And I
Cry out.

A hedge
Of trees billows
And the notes of
Nightingales. While
Low down, sharp,
Louder than all, comes the
Shrill fife
Of a
Piercing wren.

From *The Darkness and the Spring*

L'AIGUILLE DU MIDI

The peak
Rose up
Like a splinter – the
End of a pencil – to
Twelve thousand feet. And

The telepherique took us
Up
To the tip of it: just

Above the clouds.

*

Down below
Were primroses at
The winter
Wood's edge – bright
As curd, yellow as pats of
New, fresh butter – against the
Grey-brown
Woodland, and the fields'

Winter grass (grey still – though
Now their
Snow has gone).

Then – seen from our
Closed-in
Compartment of the train:
Slopes, mounting to
Snow: rock faces
Near us: valleys, wide as
The arms outstretched: all

Ending, high up, in
A grey cloud-mist
Above – which made
Everywhere
Below it a

Grey day.

Up went
The telepherique, from Chamonix
Toward the mountain's
Unseen major
Presences – turning the
Small town
Into a precisely
Modelled toy and

Widening, each way,
The long
Passage of the valley.
Up: widening the
World – and
Opening, upward, the enlarging

Mountain sides
Around us. Up

And into cloud. Mist
So thick you could only see
The suspending
Cable for ten
Yards – whereupon it
Wore away. Snow

Sometimes
Below, and a
Little rock: then that too
Is blown away. We are
Nowhere: inside our glass
Cage, in a grey
Semi-darkness.

Snow again, and
A little rock, seen through a
Rift in the grey blanket, and we are

Out:
Up – alighting
On the needle, like

A seagull on
A post
Out in the sea.

*

Mont Blanc mounts –
An immensity
In mist – near us
On one side.
To the north

Extends a
Sea of cloud, roundly
Billowing, an easy
Floor (beneath which

Are the lake, the long train
Journey here to
Buried
Chamonix, and our
Telepherique ascent): only the tips

Of the Dent du Midi's
Molar above it, like
A boat,
Afloat.

While to the east and
South a world
Of upward
Splinters opens (not just
Steep

Roof-tops – steeples, too sharp for
Snow: which heaps up
Underneath
Them) away
To the horizon: a cold

Honey-coloured – innumerably
Numerous, and great.

Exaltation! This gives
Life, at last, its longed
For – its true –
Scale. Air, snow and granite,
Altitude
And size!

The rock – strata are
All
Upward: vertical. Only
The snow
Lies: hardening, as it
Heaps, to
Ice. Ice shows,
Blue-green
A little way beneath

Me – where a fold
Of the soft down-rounding white
Has broken (to
Expose it)
In a sheer

Cliff: below which
Is space
Only, cloud, and
Beneath that

Space again.

The air's
Thinness adds a further
Vertigo

Of its own to
The precipitiousness
Of the place – and everywhere the
Dazzling, dizzy glare
Of white.

Breathless!

The clouds' sea
Stretches – two
Hundred yards
Beneath me. The vertical

Needle – granite, split – ascends
Above, yet a few further
Hundred feet, to
Its point: monolithic.
Close about, and immediately

Below, is
Snow: piled up at
This, the mountain-range's
Northern
Precipice-edge, till
It is
Ice (and
Descending on
The further, southern,
Side in sweeps
And sweeps
Of white across
The shoulder of Mont Blanc

To Italy).

While around
Is the world of peaks
Outside the world – above
It: larger than
Anything that's
In it.

Severity of
Granite, snow,
Icy clear air, ice!

The pettiness of our world's
Acceptable – if it
Is crowned, above,
By magnitude,
Immensity, like this.

Down the sheer
Face of the needle, below,
Three birds – black, with
Ragged wing-tip – wheel
Slowly, borne up
By the upward
Stillness of the air.

And between me and the
Sun (which, faint,
Shows through
A higher mist or
Curtaining of cloud – hiding away
That greatest
Seniority, which looms

Unseen:
Mont Blanc) minute

Upward-floating
Particles of snow
Sparkle, like
Infinitesimal, tingling
Fireworks, in the quiet clear

Exaltation
Of the air.

LOVE

From *The First Morning of The World*

FIRST LOVE MAKING

She was a sea.

Darkness of that
Bed: room: cottage:
Night.   Like the full
Lingering moon,   for
The first time
My mouth met
Lips' rose
In a kiss.   So

Began
my freedom: that warm
Astonishing extent of
Skin's touched
White, right out to
The horizon
Of her – of me.

Wading in the
Size, the movement, of
Her breasts – which with
Unbelievable
Fluidity and fullness
Heaped me with
Their abundance, and escaped
Then into
Flat water
Like a fish – I

Drowned, next, in her
Haunches: as she and I
Broke over one another.

And in the
Confusion of it all (drowned
Already, I hardly was
Aware of it) my man
Slipped in – to

What was so
Large and
Easily open, moist, it hardly
Seemed an
Entrance: and there

No doubt his
Abused
Stiffness was undone.

A pity
I was so
Ignorant: of her, of
Women, of what sex
Is.   I was

Hers
For all my days
Could I have eased her
Guilt for her, her contradictions,
And so helped her to
Hold to me, to teach and
To indulge me (she
Was older than
I was: old enough to
Be grown up).

Even now that darkness,
And those breasts'
Movement, like
An unsettling
Sea, move

Me.   Enslaved entirely
To that freedom's
Joy
Within her I
Could have been: as though
Not my man
But I
Myself
Has slipped into
And lived within
Her darkness: in its
Moving seas of

Complete pleasure.

Her print is
left.   Alas that

That is all.

From *Remembrance of Venus*

We are no longer
Lovers; there is
No rain of touch, no
Lake of living
In love, together; no sea in
Which we turn, at night,
Deep beneath
The surface of
one another – no naked
Sea – there is no wave

Of your hair upon
My pillow. But

Streams run underground
From Alps beyond
The horizon – past, and
Perhaps in our future – so that
The land is
Green which we walk in
Together, full
Of flowers.

                   *

If you
Were not, the world
Would be a port-less
Sea: aimless
Fluidity – a drop,
Like a tear, in which no
Image
Stood. You are

My home – my ambition: my
Adventurous
End. Were there

Not you, cancelled
Would be the earth's
Significance: out
I should sail to
Nothing, nowhere, and return
Nowhere. I
Should lose
Myself: be without
Edge, object, ease,
Security.

But – you are: that
Is inscribed clear
On the sky. And
Whatever depths

My nature has, however far
I run through time
Or shift
in space – you reach
As far, extend as
Deep, and in your

Palm receive
Me: take my
Desire, my most ambitious,
Outrageous
Extremity of feeling – and
Place it

In your place: 'Love
Enter here.'

Thus, the inmost
Jewel within
Me has
A setting: and glows, set in
It, in you,
Constant and serene.

*

She could desire,
Did: indeed, could not
Not do
So: though she

Would conceal it
Beneath friendliness, and casualness, and
Pretending that
To go naked was the natural thing to do. So I,

Admitted to her bed, assumed
The rites of exacting
Venus were established; and pursued her
Night by night across the
Calendar – till she

Broke free:
Broke me.

*

After twenty years
Her breasts are as full, as deep, as
When first I knew her
And they graced our bed: leant
Down her sides, or mine –
Heavy, like her blue-black hair which

Now is partly white. They then

Made me her maddened
Insatiable
Captive, fighting
Always like a fountain to
Reach the summit and die and
Rise again. An easy waist

Tucked her, neat,
Together: like deep
Snow the soft warmth of
Her shoulders fell; her hips

Were pear-shape – and each step
She took suggested the desperate chamber
To which her flesh compelled me and
In which I fought,
Enfolded in the warmth
Of love and kindness and our cottage and
Its candle-light. Still

I could be compelled to stir
Towards her by the white
Of her smooth clear skin, sheer, disclosed from
Head to foot – which astonished
Out desire and, laying bare
My feeling, left me
Without defence. Still
Those breasts could command
Me, by their each small
Movement, to flutter like a butterfly
Within her dark and heavy
Moving warmth. Still

She might make of me a hand
Fitted only to that glove which
She could draw
Assuaging over me, after that provocation
Of her hand-commanding
Breast. Still – yet

She left me these twenty
Years ago: preserving
Affection only. And over

Her a hardness like a rind
Has formed, which seems not to ask
A lover. While I
Have lost touch with those labyrinths
Of her feeling in which
She lost her way and I
Was her young
Ravished captive – exacting, ignorant.

Her flesh still
Is soft – her skin
As smooth. But now we
Know our difference.

Yet, did you venerate
The loveliness of Venus
In you and, through all her wide, white plains
From the stemmed-back
Mountains of her riches leap
To the act – how I in
Middle age, conquered,
Might worship her
In you!

*

The candle flame, like a stuff
Turned the cottage room's kindly walls
To curtains – stirred by
Folds of shadow as
Air moved the flame: all

Light in the room hooked
To that little wick
Beside her bed. She stood

Naked at the narrow window,
Leaning on the broad
Window-ledge – looking out
At the moon and willows and the soft
Plain: which, scented, brushed
Away to
The mountain (hidden in
Darkness: like a touch). My sight

Touched her from heel to
Head, in that candle's light. Her bed
Was white and open for her
To enter: she
For me. Exposed

As the moon, her breasts hung
Like the long swell of a
Wave, their nipples
Evident as the
Moon's clear sphere or
What rose
From me, at their sight.
Her hips were a clear line
From waist
To knee: the belly full
Before, like her
Asking lip.

Courtyard after courtyard
Of your temple

I could have entered
Till, in the shrine itself, I poured the
Sacrifice: had Venus stood
Honoured above the altar – not
Been trodden, disrespected, in the
Everyday
Dust beneath your feet. But

As you turned, your eye's
Evasion and its directness, both, denied
The goddess. Sensuality here is an
Ignored, shamefaced
Thing – not treasured, for
Its high
Virtue, in modesty's
Rich dress. The candle

Blew out the
Scene, I left
The room. Alone.

Her white walls possess
Themselves, in sleep.

From *A Dozen Portraits*

TWENTY YEARS

When I first saw her
(through a crack between the curtains)
I saw the new moon:

New moon – in a
Clear sky – of a young
Woman, twenty-seven.

A year later, was the
Full moonlight
Of her bed:

Full moon revealed, full
Woman –
As her nightdress slipped.

Those octaves opened which I
Had not known were there: a woman
Woman; depth so deep that

I, once entering, could not, would
Not
Shift away, as my roots struck

Down, deeper than I knew depth
Was – beyond sight, beyond care for the mean self's
Preservation – and my tree trunk

Stood: became my whole self, based
In her. All that, she was to me – and
Simple joy

In love, and in love
Making. Never before, for me
Had stood so wide those doors – and

Without curtain, open. She withdrawn.
What should I be – but a man
Shut from himself.

*

I love to see a lovely
Face, beauty alighted – alight within
A woman – and grow out in an

Ivy of desire about
A clear body, rounded upon warm inner
Darkness, like the earth … How is she

This, all this (so that I expect the streets
To bend toward her with desire to
Enter, as we

Walk among them, arm in arm), after now nearly
Twenty years? Her moon
Is full – and to me

Full exposed. It has its altering
Seasons: but is no more buried from me,
Fitfully, by separating circumstances'

Cloud.
Our house flowers
With the flowers she
Each day places, here and there,

About it. Are they
Hers –
Or her?

From *The First Morning of the World*

NOT A LOVER QUITE

I'll not deny that
Still, now, when I
Think of
Her: of her
Presence close
Beside me, a light
Heavy darkness, of that
Fine skin,
Of those breasts'
Grandeur – ever concealed

From me, mysterious, like the
Buried sun in
Cloud, which I never
Saw, nor knew
The true and heavy
Contour of, the
Softness: when I
Think of

The ease we
Had together
As time slipped
Transparently, slid
By, timelessly
Short (a flower one
Inch
Across): I'll not deny

That, when
I think of her, spring
Sparkles

In my veins, the landscape
Lights, peony's
Red bud

Rises, thick, through the
Dark moisture of
The soil, and my thoughts leap

One upon another, light
As nothing, above the bucking
Billows of the land.

I become love's
Acrobat – who never did

Make love to
Her (I never touched
Nor saw her
Nipple
Kindle, or put
Down – across white
Plains – a hand
To where the
World ends and
In darkness
Is the door: Still less

Entered, with that
Slipping axle which
Dear god
Answers all): nor wished

In fact
To. Yet I

Also, evidently, at
Least in fancy
Did. And evidently –
More merely
Fancifully now

Still – still
Do!

From *Next*

RELUCTANT DIVINITY

When, for my first
Love – I was very
Young – I prepared in
Our room for
Her return after a
Short
Absence, a table

Of flowers,
In effect
An altar: and

When, once, I
Scattered in our
Bed, as I turned
Back the covers
To receive
Us, a handful
Of red
Rose
Petals (they had just
Been upon the
Point of
Falling): those gestures

Embarrassed
Only. The clumsy

Flowers (a green-brown
Orchid, great winter
Anemonies like
The British flag,
And others at the
Furthest reach of my
Stretched young

Pocket) looked
Foolish, as though they
Too were
Embarrassed: while

The red rose
Petals she
Swept, scratched, out
Of the bed
In a passion of
Distressed confusion.

I had said too
Much. And
Badly. I had
Named the
Goddess.

What was it that
Distressed her? Love,
Passion, thus
Open? Less

Would more have
Pleased
Her – and less
Concealed among
Other things, not
Naked. She

Felt cornered.
Frightened. Thrust
Into undesired
Divinity.

From *Age: Abundance and the Exit*

ARUM

The arum lilies
In my yard
Sing for you,
My love. One,

Two, three, now
Four – a
Full chorus,
Unexpected, in this
Early spring.

One white
Whorl – with
Pistil-phallus (a light, sentient,
Downy
Pollen yellow) sheathed
Within. 'Lilies

Of love', you
Called them. I

See what you mean …
Thronging up
Like thirsting geese;
Trumpets blowing,
Triumphant, to the
Glory of
The lord – risen
Dark through the green
Shield shape of
The leaves – they will

Be ready for you
When you come, next
Weekend; five, six
Perhaps. The

First, which
Opened for
You, just, when you
Last were
Here, may be by
Then a little
Tiring – but
The rest, that
Have raised their chorus
Since! Each has,

At the whorl's
Tip, a
Twisted back long

Point, tinged
Green … like love's
Finger's
Touch – which
Delineates you

When we are wrapped
Together
In the bed's
White

Whorl; brow, features,
Breast, belly's gentle
Snow, striding
Thighs, to
The toes'

Conclusion; while within

All is
My home; the
Arum
Herself. In which

I am,
The whole

Of me,
Held, sheathed.
Taken.

Gone.

WIFE AND WIFE

And my darling, my
Darling, I – in
Our house
Here
Still – ask how it

Is for
You: dead (as
They say) these

Eight
Years? How?

      *   *   *

You step
Down and
Reassure me, hand upon
My shoulder; body,
Breast, pressed as
Ever up
Against me, against
My chest.

I kiss the
Gown that
Was yours, hung
Up on
The door, here
In this house
That is
Yours, you: greet your

Photograph – as
Ever on the
Mantelpiece – open
The small box

Before it containing
Treasures
Of yours: rings. Your
Wedding ring
Among them.

*   *   *

Two worlds
There are: yours –
And

This. In
This I

Have another
Love – since
I am left, surprised,
To live on
In it. Which

Does not
Deny, but
Confirms
My love for
You. Do not

Ask me
How. Inarticulate, the
Understanding is in
Each of
Us. Blessed

All
Three. Do not ask
Me how.

BEING

From *The Darkness and the Spring*

POINT

What is the point? No answer to
That question. There are no

Words – are no ideas – in which to
Frame an answer. But unless

You ask: 'What is the point?' – there
Is none. Take down the

Doors, the walls: look out, on
All sides, upon

Darkness.
Freedom!

No answer: but – now
You are alive.

*

Unless I ask
'What is the point
Of life? Of my life?'; unless I ask

'What is death? What am I,
Dead?'; unless I want to ask
These questions and, asking, find

Myself in darkness,
I cannot write
Anything worth writing. The point

Is outside all. Seeing it, dark – in
The darkness – we see it
Everywhere. Seen – there is nothing

To be said, or done, about
It. Simply, the significance of
Things

Alters. Everything has
Point. Any thing whatever is
Worth writing

*

Look out on dark, and
Breathe – at last.
Fill your lungs.

This is the scale of things! We have
Room to move. There is all that
To move

In! Seeing it, makes no
Difference – the world stays
As it was: yet

Finality
Is here: this is the
End. We

Could go away now.

*

If you cannot point and say: 'This
Is the point' – what
Is the point

Of anything at all?

Everything rests
On This: takes
From This its
Meaning.

Be very careful how
You name
It – even, conceive
Of it. Any name
Is used for
Many purposes: so every
One
Misleads. While a

Concept
Constricts: and this is
Not constricted. Best

Point. 'That is the point – in me
Here: there
In the world.' Obvious!
So obvious, it

Makes one laugh: clear
As morning
As an angel!

From *The First Morning of the World*

SNOWDROP

One snowdrop
In the garden.

The first blackbird
Sings, white, when
It is
Almost light …

The sky is
Almost blue; the sun
Yellow, almost: almost it
Powders a
Goldness
On the air.

The dark, damp, dirt
Of winter – almost is
Spring. Almost there
Is blossom, leafage, everywhere.

Take what
Denying camouflage
It may, heaven is
In us – and will

Out; in
A snowdrop. Blackbird.
Joy.

From *Age: Abundance and the Exit*

AUTUMN AFTERNOON

Calm, quiet:
Autumn. One

Cobea
Bloom, the last,
From pale
Lemon green blushes
A deep
Purple, high up
Where I can't
Reach it, in our

House wall.

In the park; long
Sun, leaves
Yellowing. Small, bright

Coloured, people stroll
Between the trees; lit
By the long
Intensely
Bright, kind, gentle –
Slanting, seeking –
Unseasonable
Sun. A

Lombardy poplar, straight
Up; its brush-tip
Hardly stirring against
The untouched
Wholeness of the
Sky's pure
Blue. And

A cock sparrow
In a bush
Preens the fluffed out
Feathers of his chest – a
Pale grey
Ball – beside the last

White roses.

At such a moment
One sees
Through a crack in
The mass, weight, density,

Confusion, complexity
Of things to
A still

Paradise; the
Truth. Don't
Move. Don't

Touch it!

From *The Ice and the Orchard*

A DAUGHTER'S GARDEN

A washing line
Runs across the garden, hung
With the minuteness of childhood.
Above it and
The grass and flowers – among the
Suburban
Sea of gardens – curves

Up, to a great height,
An apple tree: in the
Spring, a gracefully
Down-giving
Cumulus

Of dense pink
Buds, and paling
Open blossom, set in
A white fur
Of appearing
Bud-points; and

In autumn
Dropping apples red
Like out-of-season strawberries
Into the neglected grass.

From *The Glory Before the Dark*

SUMMER STORM

It's going to rain.
A storm
Will soon burst
On us and wash
Us, cool. The air

Is thick and moist,
Movement has become
An effort, and
Greyness mounts
Up higher,
Nearer, without form or
Definition – but most
Present – at
One side of the sky.
Streets
Are oppressive.

It is as though
Time had got
Stuck – as if we
Were glued
Here, in some
Dense medium
Close packed
Round us – and
Could get
No further.

We stay
Suspended.

From *The Glass of Truth*

TICKET

Returned to
My old rough
Hotel, as if
To a lost
Family, after
An absence of
Some years, I
Get up
Late, in this
New
Old place (all my life

Washed away except
For this, as though
I were already on the
Clean swept floor
Of some final
Unearned
Heaven), sit

In the silence
Of an early Sunday
Morning and
Look out of the window.

The high line of the hill
Above the City's houses
Stands as before, fringed
With snow
Along the summit, a
Grey sky
Roofing all
Immediately
Above it; while beneath

The window the
Rhône
Rushes out from
The cold lake, muscled with the
Sliding rough tumbling
Speed of its escape. Seagulls.

Laundered perfect
For the exact
Eye's pleasure, litter
The still area of air
Above the water with a
Variety of
Movement, like
Purposeful blown
Scraps of paper: and
Precipitated in careful
Lines, perch on
Horizontal railings.
While winter trees
Stand, transparent,
Still
As mist. This

Is indeed
The first
Morning of the world –
And I am
Witness
Of it.

Here is the whole
Of everything that
Is: is
Everything

That matters.

You may say: 'A river,
Seagulls, Sunday morning:
What is so particular, so
Precious, about
That?'

Here I hold all
Heaven in my hand – to
Put it down upon
A page and give it
You. A pity

I can't get through the
Barrier between
Us. Quite soon (one cannot

Live for ever) I'll have
To quit this
For some
Other place – leaving
Behind a lifetime's
Pile of these unused
Free
Entry tickets to
Heaven on this earth. If

You can't accept them, that
Is God's
Business. A pity,
I say: but only
With my small
Human voice. With my
true voice I
Say: this
Predicament that I am
In, this too

Is heaven. An
Extreme paradoxical
Exquisite refinement
Of it – shot
Through with irony

And laughter.

*

If I could but
Show you this
Morning that I
See outside my window,
Could but show
You that
This, this morning,
Is: and that you,
You, you – part of
It all – are
In heaven!

I do not want,
If I can help it,
To be here in
Heaven on
My own. However, if

This ticket that I
Write you is
Illegible –
Incomprehensible, says
To you
Nothing – then
I suppose I must.

I have spent my life
Trying (see
Heaven
Here!) to make
The inner
Outer. Here – I

Say, pointing – is
Heaven: in that
Bird, high, skating the
Sky: in that
Dewdrop on
Its chance
Blade of grass: in
The morning: any
Common fact.

Since I am then
Not only in the
World but also
Out of it, a life spent
To no effect –
A life's work
Wasted, as they
Say – does not
Destroy me. Indeed

It prepares me for
Going on doing this
Same thing, or its
Equivalent, after
Life is over.

Yet the world's
Not served. I
Have not shifted it on
Its base an
Inch. I have gone
Too far out
From it and lost my
Leverage.

That is though
After all in
The nature of the case.
To bring heaven here
You must speak
Angelic
Language: and that
Is understood
By angels
Only. So
You frustrate yourself ...

Accept that.

The alternative? To
Speak instead the

World's speech.
And so change

Nothing either.
Except yourself. Speak
That speech and
You'll lose your
Inner man.

For nothing.

From *The First Morning of the World*

APRIL IN GENEVA

I walk to work
Early in the morning, in
This extraordinary April

When the mountains are white still
Round the town, powdered with
Frost-snow to
The foot, and the air –
Even when it
Is not
Snowing – nips
The fingers.

This morning, sun
Was out.   And – when
I passed, as I do
Each day, a stretch of
Grass, mown short some
Time last autumn – blunt

Primroses were in
Flower, like
Cheerful children (each
Clump a
Slowly exploding
Firework through these last
Spring weeks), yellow
As cows'
Kindness, as the
Slap of butter.

Look again; there are
Too
Violets, so dark and
Close to the ground that
They are hardly
Noticed; fresh as
Some impossible night's

Recesses in
The eye of day, of
A shape
Indecipherable till you are
Close on them.

But that, but
That was
But the
Least of it.   On

The grassblades everywhere,
In this early morning
Unexpected sunlight of
A spring long
Overdue, were

Dewdrops (or drops of
Melted snow) which
Each one
Shone – gleamed, glinted,
Like cut
Precious stones – with
Startlingly
Different colours: suddenly
Altering as
I, moving, altered my
Angle
To them
And the sun; the sky

Held, a fiery
Moisture, in
Each drop.

New worlds, glories,
Angels!   And

I walked on to work.

Among such
Glories our
Common life is lived.

From *The Glory Before the Dark*

GLASS OF WATER

Only sometimes
Do you see what
IS: when some how

A silence
Descends
Within you and,
Through whatever it
May be that is
There
Before you, heaven
Is drawn
Clearly, as if
With a deliberate
Pencil. In this

Stillness, silence,
What is there
Before you becomes
Transparent
To that. This is

Reality: the
First – final
Moment.

*

My writing life
Is half a century's
Record of
These moments.

Enter that
Finality,

That reality, by the
Door of any
Page, no matter
What leaf, of my
Life's thick
Notebook.

*

So what you think
I'm offering
You – this still
Moment – is
Just a glass of water?

Very well.

But what is there at
The end of
Everything to offer
Anybody but

This: this raindrop,
Dewdrop,
Diamond – this
Clear pane?

After you've done
All the things in
Life that seem
Necessary, and right –
Then

What? You are
Rich perhaps,
Respected, healthy,
Loved. But
What does that
Amount to, say,
When you are

Dead – as you
Will be? In

Everything that you
Do – that you make,
Are, become – this
Glass of water, this
Dewdrop, is
the point. If

You can
Find that (here
It is –
Look!)

Keep it
Treasured: let
It become
You. This is
Your heaven, paradise,
Nirvana. No need

To look
Further. Just
Go on in
The day to day
Existence that is
Packed all
Round you – with
This

In your veins!

From *The Wound*

EVERYONE IS OUT

The stillness.

Nothing in this
Room
Stirs. The window's
Uprights and angles. Flat
Table top. Still,
All.
Silence.

Outside, a
Lombardy poplar
A field away stands
Upright, without
Motion. The world's

Suspended, in a
Silent
Heaven. Snow

Stretches across the garden,
Weighs heavily down
The hedge
Top (young
Tree trunks standing
Suddenly up out
Of it), and

Distance is
Wiped out, as if it
Never was, by
Haze.

Silence. And throughout
Myself is
Silence. Stillness.

Just now and then the
Note of a bird
Outside: or, in me,
An idea.

Empty or full – can
You tell which it
Is when
You are looking at a
Glass of water?

From *The First Morning of the World*

THE CLEAR LIGHT

I do not see why
Approaching death

Should make me say this
Heaven is not which

All my life
I have seen

Clear
As a glass of water.

From *Age: Abundance and the Exit*

FLOWER

An angel came and
Said to me: 'This,

This! This! This
Is the
End: completion!
You could
Go
Now. This is

The centre, height, is
Grandeur, splendour,
Space and scale,
Sweetness: the
Beginning, end –
Finality. Is
Being

Itself. Taste

It!
BE!

This flower – do
Not lose
It, held
Still now in
Your hand: plucked,
Between your fingers.

This is what
You are here
For: to celebrate
This – to

Put it down.'

DEATH

From *The First Morning of the World*

THE BLIND SUICIDE

Look, it's
Simple: the
More there are of
Us – and the more of everything

We use, each
One of us, destroying the earth
To get from it what we
Think we
Want – the less

Room there can be
For the rest
Of nature to
Exist: on this
Earth, which is limited.

Already the
Wild world's
Shrunk: to what? to
Half its size? The forest's
Felled; and every day some
Slow creation of a
Million years, some species –
Animal, plant or
Insect – its living area
Narrowed down to nothing,
Dies: for ever. Thus we

Cut away at our
Wild brothers'
Branches, at
The branches of the
Rooted, single tree
Which we, and they are
Together.

It might be best
For this lovely world of
Which we are a
Part – which bore, and which
Contains us – if we
Men
Destroyed one
Another, but that

We have invented ways
Of doing so now
Which would destroy
Much of the
Live earth
With us. Snuffing ourselves
Out, we'd wreak a worse,
Wider more

General last destruction.

*

Have not other creatures,
Beasts, plants – soil,
Stones even – the
right to
Be
In their own way? And

Since we're strong,
Is it not for us, who can afford
It, to recognise
That right, and to
Protect it –
From us? We must

Be now our
Mother nature's
Husband: husbandman.
Or – her small
Son still – we'll
Become her
Destroyer.

*

Let us restrain, restrict
Ourselves: allow nature
To live, in a
shared world, in her
Own way. Let us live

With
Her: not
Grab what we
Think we want, like
Little boys, but

Learn, as in making love,
Slowly our
Needs from
Her needs – from her.

Can we not see what
Is so
Simple? are we indeed

As stupid as what
We are doing seems
To show we
Are: led
By the nose, which we cannot
See beyond – helpless to

Control the
Tiger of the trivial
Desires that we are
Mounted on, which will
Devour all
Living things
Progressively, and
Us?

Can we not love our
Neighbour creatures
In this life – and find
Our joy in that?

Is there, alas!, no way,
Dear life, to stop this
Assassinating
Suicide, mankind: who, more
Even than
The rest of nature, is

Myself, my brother?

From *The Darkness and the Spring*

COURAGE FOR THE COLD

What courage have you
For that cold, now – now
You are young? What
Treasures do you lay up

For it, now: in the
Way that, in our
Middle age, we lay up
Treasure for our children? What do

You realise – in
Life – that will remain
Real, when
There is none? What do you do

With this short life, to make
Ready for that long
Journey? What glory
Do you gather, like a

Bag of seed, to
Scatter – that it springs
Up, in its season, about
That immensity, those spaces?

The end is not an end –
If you have found
The end
Already. Can it matter

That life's circle
Closes, if you have
The centre? If you have
That – what

Life will sprout
Out from it:
In life, and
After!

DEATH IS?

1.

Our knowledge – prick of light –
Binds the addict to that vast dark room
Which we might faintly apprehend without it.

The intellectual man is, thus,
A dazzled baby

Whom his wife leads by the hand.

2.

Death is
A translation. We live
In English: next is
The next world's

Arabic: a tongue
Unknowable. Yet the sense, the soul's
The same – and flowers,
Exactly rendered, in that
Unimaginably strange
New language. The sealed

Seeds of identity –
Which throws up
Birth, youth, age, embryo –
Remains, in the next

Life, let's call it.

3.

At your death – are you,
Or is the world,
Snuffed out? I see

Him die – snuffed:
The world remains, I
In it. But he?

He surely then sees
World, light, all others
Gone: himself
Remaining

At the other side of the curtain.

All *we* can say
Is that the curtain drops. This side

Of it is large
Beyond imagining? So then, too,
The other.

The curtain drops. We know;
'This corpse is dead': 'His
Life is over.' Not: 'He

Is not.' He alone could
Know that – thus: 'I
Am not.'

The curtain drops.

This
Side of it
The small chamber.

Death
That noble door
Through which our being goes,
Sloughing off all accident,
All surface, to assume

New –
Or none.

From *The Elder Brother*

II.ii

One foot is
At an angle, just
Not natural. His hair

Seen from this
Unusual point
Of vantage, thick still,
Has receded
Further than I knew. The
Clothes – worn, seemly – are
Such as he wears
At home, working,
In the day time

My dear
Boy – who are
Not this
So familiar
Body on the floor, but divorced

Suddenly and
Absolutely
From it –

Good journey: out in
That blank
Which, dwarfing us,

Does not
Diminish you!

This corpse, still
Lifelike (at the funeral,
Very dead), by its
Similitude to life
And abrupt
Lack of it, makes
Your life and
You

Present to me with
A violence
That they – and every other
Thing in our existence –
Should always
Have had, should have
At every moment: and only

A death, thus, makes
Us, for a moment,
Alive enough to feel.

The pain is
Realisation of
Your life, and you –
And of the scale

Of death.

We are made by this to
Be, almost, the
Size we are; and

The pain of being
Stretched to that
Almost kills
Us, too.

III.i

If you had gone to Australia, it
Would have been the same:
Except

That we could have
Communicated, might have
Met again, and that your

Life would have
Gone on – put out new
Leaves and branches, changing
Somewhat
Its sum: whereas

Now it
Will not.

I should have felt your
Existence, as I do
Now: felt your love, as
I do now; felt you
There – not far, nor near, yet

With me.

And our past together
Would be
As it is. The
Past is a

Perduring thing, imperishable, in
Me; in you; and
In the world. It has
Not gone: no need for
Us to
Mourn
For it.

Yet –

John
My brother
This earth that I still

Live on is hollowed
Out, pitted, pock-marked
With holes, with the
Hollows where you
Were: as though some great

Plant species had everywhere been
Rooted from the earth.

No more, in spring,
Will aconites and snowdrops come
By post to us from
You, in small pipe-tobacco
Tins, half filled with
February moss – out of that

Great neglected garden: grown back to
English jungle (except for the lawn

Before the housefront under
Apple trees – blossoming
In spring, and dropping
Winter apples – and the
Thickening catalpa that once
Was full of children).

That house itself
Must soon be
Sold: one woman, alone, can not
Live in it.
The life you held up
Here – for yourself, and
With us – must all be

Taken down.

It is extraordinary,
Inconceivable, that I shall
Never now
Sit at your hearth again, with you there

Sitting in that chair.

But
The past: is

Within us. The
Present is where

We live: I
And you too.

IN OLD AGE

I'll get impatient in old age if
I'm kept long, waiting in
That draughty passage
At the exit.

The horizon narrows,
Habits harden, a scrub
Of worrying detail fills the foreground
Keeping the wide world out. Sunk self-
Deceptions and deficiencies – seen last
Exposed in childhood, and
Submerged since
By the full flesh of life –
Are revealed again like rusty bicycles
Below the tide line as the untidy sea
Draws out; set themselves, brittle,

Against the cold
Intractability of fact.

FROM AN AEROPLANE

I look down
Past the wing edge
At the small scratched fields of France
And torn fluff-scraps
Of intermediate cloud. High up,

Free: in light, ease,
Brightness. Is death
This –
Liberation? Or is it

To be deep in, in
The solid dark: pressed close
Within solid
Substance, on the
Inward side of things: packed back,
Moveless, in mother – unchanging, in
What was before?

No. It is to
Be divested
Of everything we know, of all for
Which there's concept: all
Clothes – and
To be dressed in new
There is now no
Word for
In our wardrobe.

I meditate upon death
Much, as a boy might
On his manhood. Something great
I sense there is in things – which makes
Existence here, to that
Boy's eye
Look childish. These
Clothes – his
Short trousers – sit
Somewhat uncouth and

Gawky on me, like a splitting
Sepal: as though I had been

Wrapped up
Inexpertly, in a by-now
Rather battered
Parcel – some time soon

Ready for delivery.
You may be sure however that
Whatever changes then I
Shall remain – like
A boy grown up
Myself. And
Foolish. So, from this plane

At Geneva will
Step out the same
Tiresome man my wife this morning,
In our bed, released
From her arms wrapped round him.

She is the dress that
Fits me closest – close
Almost as my
Self's skin. Yet even we,

Thus practise our parting.

From *A Marriage*

I have just been
Strolling in the
Gardens
Opposite our house (where

We walked, in
All seasons, among
The playing children and
Antique tombstones) on a

Bright October day,
Through whose
Cool invigorating
Air the kind sun's
Warmth is
Drying up
The minute
Attentiveness of dew
On the short
Grass: each

Drop of it an
Altering
Gem stone, if
One moves one's
Angle to
The light. (As you
And I my love,
My love, this
Morning!)

Leaves fall like a
Flutter of pigeons
In any
Breath of wind
And lie
Dry – brilliant browns

Of cut-out
Leaf shapes – on
The lush
Grass's vivid
Green. Across the

Trees, onto pools of
Smooth-mown
Grass, in a slight
Mist the sun
Slants: so every
Thing it strikes
And one's eye
Lights upon is
Beautiful as
If in
Paradise. In

Everything one's eye
As it happens
Rests upon
Paradise
Is here.

*

Dew on short grass
In sunlight
First we saw
Together once in
Wales. A small

Handkerchief of lawn,
Private – up the
Mountain's side. You
Sat half-stripped
And sunned
Yourself – thirty-five,
Forty years
Since, was
It? – in that

Dew jewellery and
Silence.

Since then many
Dews and raindrops, many
Suns and scenes have
Come, shifted, gone.
And we have moved

Among them: like the
Few people in
These gardens
Today – seen beyond
Shade and sunlight
Through the thin
Mist, in sylvan
Islands, pools,
Of sun. […]

*

[…] Gone though you are

From everywhere about
Me – yet it is not
Your absence
But, innerly, your
Presence
That I feel …

Let me, my love,
Evoke this room
As it was when it
Was a bower of
Flowers round
You, sitting up
Against your cushions
Like a
Goddess
In her grove.

From the gardens
And hothouses of
The south of England the
Flowers
Came. Snowdrops,
Aconites and violets
First, with hothouse
Pots of large

Azaleas (these at
Intervals I stood out
In bath –
To draw
Up transparent
Water's life, which bloomed
Then in
The petals). Camellias

Too: one pale
Pink one from the public gardens
Opposite, which
Surreptitiously I
Stole, because she
Particularly
Loved it (this still
Blooms
There, a tender
Deepening pink
With no shrill
Sickliness of
Sugar); and that red

One from our
Yard: which,
Dropping, I laid
Before her
On a saucer – as
She herself would
Have done.

Jonquils next, daffodils and
Tulips. Mixed
Abundant posies. I'll not
Go on. A storm

Of flowers it was,
Precipitating on
Every surface that
Would hold
Them: mantelpiece, extinct
Stove, bookshelf
Top, the table at
Her bed
End, and the
Bed-tray slung

Across her knees: on
Which was ranged her
Narrowed life of
Minute meals and
Tea and radio
And things that
She might read.

Queen enthroned she
Sat up
There, weakening as
Spring gained
Strength: the frequency
And length of her
Friends' visits
Dwindling. It needs
Energy – an effort –
Even to be
Glad. Her

World – the nest,
The pod she was held
Treasured
In – and the
Time she was

Awake,
Contracted; while
The flowers
And occasional spring
Sunshine
Blazed. […]

                    *

[…] How many people
Have the luck to
Be given an
Hour and a half of
Quietness to say
Goodbye to
Their love
In? We said our

Goodbyes
In the calm
Warmth of that
Cherishing cocoon
Which the universe
For us had
Shrunk to. And

I – how
Many have this
Immense
Good fortune? – was
Able to tell
Her all
My love: to say what
She had
Meant to me in
More than
Half a lifetime. To be

Able
In so many
Words to say
That!

Emotionally exceedingly
Ambitious though I
Am – I said – if when
Growing up
I had tried to
Imagine what extreme
Fulfilment might
Be, I could not
Have conceived anything
Remotely in the
Region of what
I had
Known with

Her: a deep which,
In its receiving
Darkness, contained
All of
Me, and in which,
Striking out, I could
Encounter no
Restraining shore. Much

More than any
Ambition that I
Knew I had, was
In her
Satisfied: my
Life was
Full. Thanks to
Her, to what
We had
Together, there was
No more
Anything that
I needed to
Make my
Life complete.

We thanked each
Other – though that
Is a poor
Word for it. And
She, a little
Drowsy, very weak,
Looked out
At the black before
Her (black ? –
Negatives alone can
Indicate what we here
Cannot know) with
A matter of fact
Acceptance, calmly, quietly,
As being – which it
Is – in the
Nature
Of things. While I
Kissed her: for
The how many
Hundred thousandth
Time ? Held
Her hand.

*   *   *   *   *

A little time more
And the breathing
Stopped. Silence.
Peace.

*

[…] Empty, this
World: a huge
Echoing
Pointless space.
With nothing
In it.

181

The stuff of things
Is cleft in
Two. And I

Am a wound, one
Wound from
Head to foot. Flayed
All over. Each

Touch upon me
Is – touching her absence –
Pain. Nothing can

I do that
Does not
Touch the
Pain and tell me

That she is
Not here.

The centre of
My life is taken
Out, to which
All threads
Were tied – and
Hang
Slack, without
Meaning. For

Everything that I
Was and
Did, related
To her: referred
Back to
Her.

I wake in the
Morning to
Nothing at my side. [...]

*

[...] In this yard
Of ours, the gardens
Opposite, and at one
Spot in the
Park, places you
Loved, I
Scattered
Your light
Ashes.

In the park
There is an enclosed
Garden: reached
Through a courtyard.
It
Was a secret,
Private place for
You in which
The inmost
Opened; a place
Such as only a
Lover at
Extreme
Stretch could
Penetrate. There

I scattered
The last of the
Ashes.

Ashes are a small
Thing, beside all
That there is
Else. Yet
Like a sparrow's
Feather, light,
Exquisite, on the
Grass, like the light
Touch of
A finger, they say
Something which
Cannot
Otherwise be said.

From *The Wound*

CAMELLIA

Violets are out again,
My love, pushing up
Through the short damp
Winter grass.

Each year you hoped
They would be out upon
Your birthday, at the
Springing of your life:
In early
March. But this
Year, lacking you,
Already they
Are a full month
Late. Yet

At last they
Spring up – with speedwell,
Celandine: a low, early,
Inch-high
Spring. Life, life,
In them
Springs up: springs
And speaks

Existence once again.
Your existence: present
To me in these
Violets – and in

The pink camellia
In the public gardens
Opposite our
Door, which you
Loved most, and

Which flowers
First, beneath the tall
Trees there. I stole

Bloom from that to
Put up on your
Coffin as it was
Borne away: and
Now have
Picked another, which sits
Today upon
My table, in a glass
Thimble-size. The perfect

Rosette of that
Tender pink
Looks out at
Me; I can
Brush it with my
Cradling
Palm – greeting you
In the morning, at night,
And at moments
Passing
In the day.

The core, the
Innermost of you
Has not
Departed, is present
To the innermost of
Me – though I live
Out this
Vestige of my life
(Almost, to my
Astonishment, happily
By now)
Without you.

From *Age: Abundance and the Exit*

SUDDENLY LEFT STRANDED

I like it here,
In the last
Evening light after a
Hot spring day.
Sparkle

On the shadowed
Darkness of the water.

A stretch of time
Unlooked for, unassigned,
With no
Expectation
Written
On it. A present

From the lord!

What are all our
Intent
Endeavour,
Our purposes
For? Add
Them up. Well,

Nothing! The end,
Beginning, centre,
Interior of
Things is

Here.

An essence
Which is in
Death, too,
Unaltered.

*

The immense
Silence. Meaning itself

Alights. A blank
Space: wide
Stretch of
Evening water.

The sun
Hangs; slowly
Drops toward,
Misting over, the
Horizon. A drooping

Flag just
Stirs.

Difficult not to
Wipe this moment
Out, by
Filling it.

We cannot long
Sustain, arms
Opened wide the
Perfect
Moment: absence of
Everything – but
Peace.

Bliss.

PRAISE OF AGE

The shutting
Of memory's
Erratic door on the
Near and
Middle distance of
One's past is

Balanced by
An opening of
Its far
Distance: a

Many-roomed, vast
Many-storey'd
Mansion in which you

Wander as you please
With appreciation,
Gratitude – sharpened
Keen by the long
Perspective of your years.

My nursery's dark
Green
Linoleum; corner
Of our garden where
I dug down
Two inches to
Australia (wearing, I
Think, a flat
Obliterative cloth
Cap); sights
Scents
Everything that
Was then
Around me; all

Near the ground. As

I was near
That unknown
Beginning in my

Mother's bed.